LATIN AMERICAN POLITICS
IN PERSPECTIVE

MARTIN NEEDLER
University of Michigan

D. VAN NOSTRAND COMPANY, INC.
PRINCETON, NEW JERSEY

TORONTO   LONDON
NEW YORK

D. VAN NOSTRAND COMPANY, INC.
120 Alexander St., Princeton, New Jersey
(*Principal Office*)
24 West 40 Street, New York 18, New York

D. VAN NOSTRAND COMPANY, LTD.
358, Kensington High Street, London, W.14, England

D. VAN NOSTRAND COMPANY (Canada), LTD.
25 Hollinger Road, Toronto 16, Canada

Published simultaneously in Canada by
D. VAN NOSTRAND COMPANY (Canada), LTD.

PRINTED IN THE UNITED STATES OF AMERICA

TO

LORE

AND

STEPHEN

Grateful acknowledgment is made to Professor William G. Andrews for his advice and encouragement; to my wife and son, to whom the book is dedicated, for their patience and forbearance; to Miss Susan Stoudinger for her services as typist; and to the students and lay audiences in New Hampshire and Michigan who stimulated and corrected the ideas that became the content of this book.

M. C. N.

Ann Arbor
May, 1963

Contents

Introduction

WHY STUDY LATIN AMERICAN POLITICS?

It seems only fair to begin a book with a statement of the author's reasons for presuming on the reader's time. The writer on Latin America may find himself under varying degrees of constraint on this score, since public interest in the area waxes and wanes markedly in response to the vicissitudes of international politics, rising if today's crisis is a Latin American one, dropping when the headlines concern a country in the Eastern Hemisphere. Why should the conscientious North American[1] feel he ought to know what goes on in the countries to the south?

One often hears the argument: these countries are after all our closest neighbors and so should have first call on our attention; and much is written and spoken that starts out from the premise that the United States and the countries of Latin America are indeed neighbors, living next door to each other in a single hemisphere. Now this argument may have some force if one is referring to Mexico, Central America, or the Caribbean. It is rather weak, though, as applied to the countries of South America—the major cities of Brazil or Argentina are closer to those of West Africa, for example, than they are to the cities of the United States: Buenos Aires is 5800 miles from New York, and only 3000 from Dakar, Senegal; Natal, in the Brazilian Northeast, is only 1800 miles from Dakar. In fact, New York is closer to Moscow by air than it is to Buenos Aires.

---

[1] "North American" rather than "American" is normal usage, and is preferred, in the Latin countries of the hemisphere.

1

The argument that Latin America is important to the United States for economic reasons makes more sense. There is an impressive list of materials, from abaca to zinc and from balsa wood to lead, which come to this country from the republics to the south. And yet, there are sources for almost all of these products elsewhere in the world—and for all of the important ones—whereas for many of them substitutes could be developed if necessary. (On the other hand, the United States is certainly important to Latin America—it takes over half of the exports of two-thirds of the republics, and supplies over half of the imports of a similar number.)

But from the point of view of United States foreign policy, surely, Latin America is of importance just as any area must be of importance to a great state with worldwide interests and responsibilities; but the argument that the area should have some type of priority consideration, while understandable and commendable in the light of past U. S. neglect of the area, seems hardly to be substantiated.

Quite apart from its significance to the student of foreign policy, however, Latin America is, or should be, of great interest to the student of comparative politics. The existence of 20 republics of comparable culture, most of them independent for a century and a half, suggests a wealth of political experience that can be mined to yield valuable insights and fruitful hypotheses.

THE MANNER OF APPROACH

In dealing with a group of countries that have some characteristics in common, one can adopt either of two methods—stress similarities or stress differences. Each method has its strengths and weaknesses: to lay emphasis on the differences and consider each country individually involves repetition and may lose the insights that come with truly comparative work; to focus on similarities, on the other hand, means to minimize or overlook significant variations among countries and may create in the student the illusion of familiarity where there is only superficial acquaintance.

This book adopts the comparative approach, organizing the material by topics and laying stress on those features possessed in common by the countries of the area. It is the author's belief, however, that for a sound knowledge of Latin American politics a thoroughgoing acquaintance with the politics of the individual countries is necessary *in addition to* comparative study by topics; in his own teaching he has found it possible to combine both methods with encouraging results. To derive the maximum intellectual return on his investment, the reader is strongly advised, in addition, to become as familiar as possible with the geography of the area.

In following a topical and comparative outline, and in trying to do justice to the complexities of the subject within the brief compass of this book, the intention has been neither to be overwhelmed by masses of data nor to overwhelm the reader with them, but instead to use specific data as examples of principles, that is, to tie together specific material by what may perhaps pass, in the primitive state of the art, for theoretical structure. It is hoped that any sacrifice of detail that this may have entailed will be compensated for by the reader's being able to make some sense, when he finishes the book, of Latin American politics.

The focus of the book, by way of contrast to others on the same and similar topics, is on the regularities of informal political life rather than on the provisions of formal institutions of government or on the general cultural factors that relate to politics. It is the author's own feeling that this difference of emphasis helps to redress the imbalance that now exists in the literature on comparative Latin American topics.

WHAT DO THE LATIN AMERICAN COUNTRIES HAVE IN COMMON?

The differences among the countries that are considered here are substantial enough that it will scarcely be possible to make a generalization without immediately noting a list of exceptions to it. If one wished to stress the variations among the countries of the area, and not their similarities, he would have powerful arguments on his side. "Latin America," after all, includes Uruguay, whose inhabitants are Spanish-speaking, of European stock, and whose government is a stable and peaceful democracy; it includes Paraguay, a country of mixed European-Indian inhabitants who speak Spanish and Guaraní, and who have always lived under dictatorship; it also includes Haiti, where the people are of African descent, speak a dialect of French, and have lived for the most part, one has to say, in a state of anarchy; and it includes Brazil, whose language is Portuguese, and whose forms of government have been as various as the biological inheritance of its people. If Brazilians, Haitians, Uruguayans, and Paraguayans are all Latin Americans, how can one generalize? What do the various republics have in common?

Politically speaking, they share the following characteristics, among others. In the first place, they have all had the experience of being colonies of a European Power, being ruled from abroad through the agency of a class of resident foreigners who monopolized the positions of local authority. With the exception of those in Brazil and Haiti, the institutions of government were similar in all the colonies. On the whole, the republics share the geographic characteristic that communications are made difficult by natural barriers—mountains, deserts, jungle—so that the population of the countryside perforce participates little in the political life of the capital. (On this point one would have to except Uruguay and Argentina outright, while modifying its application in some other cases.) Their economies are similar in that all are dependent to a greater or lesser extent on the production of primary products—that is, agricultural or mineral products—mainly for export, and therefore are sensitive to fluctuations in international commodity prices.

In addition, the republics of Latin America share a common political consciousness, an awareness of what is happening to each other, which can make developments in one country of direct influence elsewhere. If a dictator in one country falls, the dictator of another sleeps less comfortably; the words of a great democratic leader in one republic will evoke a response in the hearts of the citizens of a neighboring state.

Finally, the states of the area are similar in finding themselves, on the whole, at a comparable stage of political development. They have all passed through the stage of defining basic constitutional structure that follows immediately on independence; they have all had to reach some kind of *modus vivendi* between Church and State; they have all had to cope with the problems confronted in passing through the early stages of labor organization. Today they are all involved—or are shortly to be involved—with the problems of trying to reconcile the processes of democracy not only with political stability but at the same time with the requirements of rapid economic growth.

It is the author's own belief that this last point is the most important of all, and that the history—in some cases, the contemporary history—of countries on other continents supports him in the view that the politics of the Latin American republics are simply the politics of states at a certain series of stages in their political evolution. The reader will find, accordingly, that the concept of "political development" recurs throughout the discussion that follows, while from time to time parallels are pointed out with the experience of states outside the area.

I   *Political Culture*

The term "political culture" has been used to refer to the totality of the factors, not themselves political, which determine the environment in which political processes operate: the traditions, attitudes, or normal patterns of behavior and thought that condition political action. The leading features of Latin American political culture considered in this chapter will be: the heritage of colonial rule, the state of those social factors that affect a country's stage of political development, and the nature of the issues that have formed the matter of political controversy in the period since independence from the colonial Power.

A. THE COLONIAL HERITAGE

It would be an error of the first magnitude, in any attempt to understand the politics of the Latin American republics, to overlook the powerful influences exerted on them by three centuries of colonial rule. Let us consider in turn the political institutions and attitudes handed on from the colonial period, the political implications of the inherited patterns of social behavior, and, finally, the role of the Church.

POLITICAL INSTITUTIONS

The political forms that the Spaniards brought to the Americas were those of a particular time and place. To appreciate this is at the same time to understand much about them. They were, after all, by and large the institutions that Spain herself had at the end of the fifteenth century; in other words, at a time of absolute monarchy, of national unification, and of the expulsion of the Moors from

6

Spanish soil. It is a nice symbolic fact that the year in which Columbus "discovered" America, 1492, was also the year in which the Moors (that is, the Muslims from North Africa and the Near East who had added the Iberian Peninsula to the empire established by the successors to Mohammed) were finally forced out of the peninsula after centuries of warfare.

The national unification of Spain took place along lines similar to those followed in the unification of the other European states of the period. This was the time of the transformation of a feudal Europe, with its sharply stratified society, its elaborate network of mutual rights and obligations, and its multitude of local rulers owing vague allegiances to King, Emperor, and Pope, into a Europe of states, sovereign and equal, each ruled by a more or less absolute monarch who worked out the terms under which the Catholic Church should be permitted to conduct its affairs within his realm, if at all.

The strategy of national unification necessarily required that the king break the power of the local lords and the traditional autonomy of their domains. In this struggle, the monarch found natural allies in the burghers of the towns; for trade would surely stand to benefit by the policy of national unification, with its concomitant abolition of the internal tariffs and arbitrary exactions of a fragmented feudal society, and its improvement of communications. In return for their aid in the common struggle, the king re-confirmed the cities' self-rule charters or granted new ones, undertook to respect the autonomy of the guilds, and perhaps granted the city representation in the councils that advised him. The nobility, for its part, would be centralized at the Court, the nobles being transformed from rivals for power into royal civil servants or soldiers, or ineffectual courtiers.

As has always happened, before and since, national unification carried with it its own ideological force, a concept of national purpose and a feeling of national vigor which, with the mission of unification accomplished, looks beyond the national borders for new tasks in which to affirm its destiny. The ideology of the new Spain, matured in the long struggle to free the national soil of the infidel, could only be a militant and missionary Catholic Christianity. With the Reconquest, then, Spain was ready to go on to conquer a new world for trade, for the royal house, for the faith. It only remained that the new world be discovered.

Amplifying the Reconquest into the Conquest, as the theater of military activity moved beyond the seas, it was natural that the institutions appropriate to the one be adapted to the other. The fusion of political and military authority forged out of the necessities of frontier government on the marches of Christian advance in the home country continued in the offices of captain-general, governor, *adelantado,* that were conferred on the men who won the New World for Spain. Together with the auxiliary task of spreading the faith, that combination was quite appropriate to the needs of conquering new lands for Spain in America.

Colonial ways have left a lasting imprint on government in Hispanic America. In the colonies political authority and military command were joined; today most of the Latin American republics have still to create a military service separated from politics. Governmental authority in the colonies, as in Spain, was highly centralized and absolute; so it is in the republics. Law was the command of a sovereign who owed responsibility only to God and his conscience; today most of the Latin American legislatures are subservient to executives that are only nominally co-equal.

As in the mother country, the town enjoyed a certain degree of self-rule, and the town council (*cabildo* or *ayuntamiento*) was the only public authority that—at least at some times and in some places —was outside the executive chain of command. Because of this, the councils necessarily figured prominently in the Independence movement and the early governments of the republics. Today, it is usually only in the cities that one finds sustained participation in political processes.

Under Spanish rule, at least until shortly before Independence, mercantilist practices prevailed, with all colonial trade oriented to the mother country and inter-colonial dealings forbidden. The separateness of the colonies thus encouraged, which reinforced the formidable natural barriers to communication, helps explain the separate existence of the republics of today, whose boundaries generally follow those of the colonial administrative divisions of 200 years ago. In addition, many of the characteristics peculiar to the populations of each of the republics can be shown to derive from variations among the regions of Spain from which the colonists of each state derived.

The independent states also inherited the colonies' responsibilities to religion, many of them continuing the special status of the Church that had existed under Spain.

Not all of present-day Latin America was under Spanish rule, however. As an eventual result of the Treaty of Tordesillas, in which the Pope arbitrated rival Spanish and Portuguese claims, and of the energy and initiative of Portuguese colonizers, the vast domains of Brazil came under Portuguese rule. Of the quality of Portuguese colonial rule, one might say in general that it rested more lightly on the colony than did Spanish rule elsewhere in the hemisphere, although the institutions of government in the two empires were comparable. The Portuguese in America, like their descendants there today, were more easy-going, less insistent on religious orthodoxy, more tolerant of local initiative than the Spaniards.

In French-ruled Haiti, on the other hand, life on the plantations was on the whole very harsh for the African slaves imported to replace as laborers the aboriginal Indians who had rapidly died out as the direct or indirect result of the severity of colonial exactions. Of course its quality varied with the character of the individual slaveowners, but the French were typically harder masters than the Portuguese. The treatment of colored freedmen in Haiti, at first generous, deteriorated as they came to outdistance the *petits blancs,* the poorer whites, in wealth and accomplishments, resulting, by the end of the eighteenth century, in an onerous system of legal disabilities, discrimination, and segregation.

The colonial mold has surely left its impress on the substance of political life in the republics of present-day America. It would be incorrect, however, to treat the nature of the colonial heritage as in itself sufficient to account for the features of politics in the area today. Characteristics of the colonial pattern that were appropriate to the changing circumstances of the republics remained, were strengthened, and were exaggerated; those that no longer had a function disappeared, or survived only as isolated anachronisms; while totally new practices grew to supply new needs. The active factors in the process were the requirements of time and place, the impact of crucial events and personalities, and the logic of the situations that developed. But much of the colonial pattern retained its relevance in the years that followed Independence: and that portion exerted its influence over the new, so that today an appreciation of the colonial heritage remains a prerequisite to an understanding of contemporary political life.

SOCIAL BEHAVIOR

The society founded by the Spaniards was, of course, a class society. The Spaniards came to conquer and to rule, not to work with their hands. The medieval conception of the nobleman whose only proper tools were the sword and the word of command was very much alive among the new arrivals in the Americas. To be sure, there was no need for the newcomers to labor, for the Spaniards conquered large bodies of sedentary people who could be put to work.

Here lies one of the crucial differences between what happened in English- and in Spanish-speaking America. The invaders from England found a few nomadic Indians not permanently settled in any one area, who could readily be driven off. At the same time, the thrifty Puritans who emigrated to the New World were ready and eager to work the new-gained land themselves. The large populations of sedentary Indians to the South, by contrast, could hardly have been expelled; and in any case the Spanish nobleman was not at all interested in doing his own farming and mining. Quite naturally, therefore, the Spaniards related to the Indians, whose land they were taking, as an upper class in a highly organized class society.

Thus, the type of society that each set of invaders found in its half of the New World was adaptable to the type of society conforming to the predilections of each. The English Puritans, independent and hardworking at home, could remain so—could become more so—in America; the Spanish *hidalgo,* or his lower-class imitator, aspired at home to the dignified and genteel way of life he found himself able to live in the colonies.

There were regional variations from this general organization of colonial society, however. In the Caribbean tropics, on the islands, and in the lowlands of the surrounding coastal areas, the Indians proved intractable as plantation workers, dying, escaping into the back country, or refusing to be captured in the first place. Here Negro slaves were imported, as they were to Brazil from the vast Portuguese African domains, and today the African strain predominates in these areas. What Indians inhabited the areas of present-day Argentina and Uruguay, on the other hand, were nomadic, and could not be made to serve as the lower class of an agricultural society. There the Indians met the same fate as those in the United States, being driven out or exterminated, and the land was settled almost exclusively by Europeans, as largely occurred also in Costa Rica.

The combination of these social factors with those of climate and terrain led to the three basic types of rural economy which, in general, one still encounters in Latin America. In the Indian-less countries of Uruguay and Argentina, one finds economies based on livestock-raising, needing much land and few workers. The tropical areas, by contrast, the coastlands of Northern South America and the Caribbean, grow plantation crops—sugar, bananas, cacao—usually on large economic units worked by the descendants of the indigenous peoples and of African slaves. Elsewhere, Indians and *mestizos* (those of mixed European and Indian ancestry) are found as workers in the mines, and on the *haciendas* (landed estates), and sometimes their own small farms, growing corn and vegetables.

The Spanish blueblood's attitude toward work is still current in the Latin countries of America. The upper-class Latin American

generally has a casual attitude toward the obligations of his job that
comes as a surprise to the North American (as anyone who has
tried to make an appointment to see a Latin American colleague can
testify!) The strength of this attitude varies from place to place, however, and the inhabitants of some of the more industrial cities of
the area pride themselves on being more businesslike than their
compatriots in the national capitals.

Similarly, the attractive careers for the Latin American student
are those involving cerebral activity only, and that of a less demand-
ing type. The universities are full of students of philosophy, poets,
and apprentice politicians. There are lawyers enough to go round,
and the supply of would-be men of letters more than meets the demand. Agronomists, statisticians, and rural schoolteachers, on the
other hand, are less in evidence. As industrialization progresses,
however—and it is well under way in Argentina, Uruguay, Brazil,
and Mexico, and beginning elsewhere—these attitudes presumably
will begin to give way.

The relatively greater importance of the family in Latin America
than in Britain or the United States should be mentioned in any
discussion of the traditional social patterns that survive to affect political behavior today. Family connections are of importance in Latin
America (as in other areas of the world, of course) to a greater
extent than in the United States, and that means not simply the
"nuclear" family of immediate relatives, but the extended family of
cousins three or four times removed. Feelings of special loyalty extend also to those related not by blood, but by virtue of being god-
parents to the other's children (*compadrazgo*). One's *compadres,*
like one's relatives, are entitled to special consideration. With this
set of attitudes, nepotism and family favoritism become regarded
as an almost legitimate obligation rather than as an illegitimate betrayal of trust. An officeholder is likely to regard loyalty to a "public interest" as a nebulous and unreal obligation that must take a
lower priority than the natural loyalty one feels to flesh-and-blood
relatives. This type of attitude is maintained and strengthened by

various functional imperatives that will be discussed below in the section on the public administration.

THE POSITION OF THE CHURCH

The strength of the Church, and of Catholic Christianity itself, varies markedly from one republic to the other. Whereas Protestantism or Judaism nowhere in the area constitute serious rivals to Catholicism (although Protestant missions are active in several countries, especially Brazil), a rival of a kind exists in Haiti, and to some extent in Brazil, in the cults derived from the primitive religions of Africa, which survive among some Latin Americans of African descent. In Haiti, Voudun retains a claim on the allegiance of probably most of the dwellers in rural areas, while the Brazilian equivalent, "spiritualism," has a substantial following among the poorest 20 per cent in the cities, as well as in the country.

Some purists have pointed out that often the Christianity of the aboriginal American is heavily dosed with practices owing their origin to religions of the pre-Columbus period. Re-baptised Indian deities have often found a place in the local Christian hagiology; while local variations in the celebration of Christian holidays are evocative of heathen practices.[1]

It remains true that loyalty to the Catholic faith is strongest in the more Indian states of America, and weaker in the more European and African. The most secular state in the region, for example, is Uruguay, with its population almost 100 per cent of European descent, where the public calendar does not even carry the religious names of the national holidays—December 25th is "Family Day!" Indian-and-*mestizo* Ecuador, on the other hand, has been called "the land of churches," and was once dedicated by Presidential decree to the Sacred Heart of Jesus (as was Peru also). The Indians'

---

[1] The skeptic might remark, apropos of motes and beams, that observations of this type are made with unconscious irony by those whose own Christmas features the fir tree of the ancient Germanic religion, or whose celebration of Easter involves such primitive heathen fertility symbols as eggs and rabbits.

loyalty to the Church may derive in part from the Church's role in protecting them, or attempting to, from the worst exactions of the civil authorities in colonial times, or it may simply reflect the greater religiosity of a primitive people living close to nature and the soil.

The political position of the Church itself has undergone considerable change over the years. One might fairly say that during the colonial period the Church was an integral part of the political-military-religious Establishment, with a role to play in the maintenance of the colonial system. As a corporate body—that is, as it acted through its formal hierarchy—the Church was a partner of the royal administration. Itself a landowner, the largest in the colonies, its bishops connected by ties of blood to the ruling classes, the Church found itself consistently on the Conservative side of issues, under Spain and in the Independence period.

The parish priests, however, lower down in the hierarchy, could identify themselves with the cause of the lower classes. The father of Mexican independence was a priest, Father Hidalgo. (Before being executed he was defrocked, however, as was his follower, Father Morelos.) One has a similar phenomenon today in the fight of Father Ramón Talavera against the Stroessner dictatorship in Paraguay, without the (overt, at least) support of his superiors in the Church hierarchy.

The identification of the Church with the forces of social conservatism, in general, continues to this day, but has been mitigated by two complementary developments. In the first place, the Church, since the "social encyclicals" of Leo XIII, has taken a position on social questions compatible with attempts to ameliorate the conditions of life of the working classes. Since the end of World War II especially, Christian Democratic or Christian Social parties have been founded, in Western Europe and Latin America, which favor the secular claims of the Church (for example, to participate in the education of the young) but which are at the same time socially progressive. Until then, one implicitly assumed that a pro-clerical political position entailed a conservative view of social and economic questions. Parties of this type have already achieved a leading position in the politics of Chile and Venezuela. In the second place, the Church has discovered that the twentieth-century dictator, in his continuing attempt to achieve ever more totalitarian authority, must sooner or later come into conflict with any organized body that remains outside the range of his control, including the Church itself. This will happen, experience has shown, no matter how favorable to the Church the dictator's initial acts will seem, nor how much the Church tries to "render unto Caesar": the totalitarian claims of modern dictatorship must necessarily end by invading the sphere the Church holds to be its own. This happened toward the end of the Perón period in Argentina, as it did during the term of Rojas Pinilla in Colombia.

Although a formal separation of Church and State exists today in several of the republics—the most important of which are Brazil, Uruguay, and Chile—the more usual pattern is for some kind of official recognition of Catholicism as the dominant religion, together with mild grants of government favor in the form of subsidies for church schools and the like. This is in normal times the situation in Argentina, Peru, Colombia, and Costa Rica, for example. In a few Latin American states, the Church has been subject to jealous vigilance and occasional persecution; in Mexico and Ecuador, for example, where the extent of anti-clerical feeling is probably a reflection of the degree to which the Church has historically attempted to intervene in secular matters; and currently in the Caribbean dictatorships of Cuba and Haiti.

One of the complaints that anti-clerical governments in the area typically make is that Church education and other activities weaken patriotism because so many clerics are foreigners (generally Spaniards; Frenchmen and French Canadians in Haiti). On the other hand, the opinion of foreign observers—since Independence especially, but even before—has been so unanimous in its condemnation of the average levels of intelligence, morality, culture, and general worthiness of their office of native priests, that one is inclined to be cautious about the merits of any program of expulsion of foreign-born clerics, on this as well as on other grounds.

B. RACE, CLASS, AND POLITICAL DEVELOPMENT

THE CONCEPT OF POLITICAL DEVELOPMENT

The temptation is apparently irresistible for the foreign observer to make quantitative and qualitative comparisons among the Latin American states. This is not an idle temptation, for much can be learned by comparison that could not have been learned any other way; at the same time, systematic comparison provides a way of ordering and organizing a large body of data so that it becomes understandable and usable. Presumably because democracy and stability are the attributes most generally held to be desirable, comparisons with respect to them are the most frequent. One distinguished political scientist and observer of the Latin American scene has conducted periodic polls among his colleagues in recent years to discover their assessment of how democratic the states of the area were in comparison with each other.[2]

A difficulty of using "degree of democracy" as the dimension in which one makes comparisons, however, is that it is susceptible of sudden and drastic change. A *coup d'état* in Cuba or Colombia may send the country from the head of the list to somewhere near the bottom; a successful revolution may move it from the bottom to somewhere near the top, literally overnight. On the other hand, stability, as a comparative measure, has the fatal weakness that there are two very different types of stability (a fact that U. S. foreign policy has very infrequently shown itself able to appreciate), that of the peaceable constitutional democracy, where revolts rarely or never occur because everyone can feel generally satisfied with the political order, and confident that it will do him justice; or the stability of the iron-fisted dictatorship, which rules by terror and

[2] Professor Russell Fitzgibbon. His article describing the results of the latest survey appeared in the *American Political Science Review* for September, 1961.

deceit, and which, last as long as it may, is likely only to serve as prelude to eventual anarchy and bloody civil strife.

Clearly, what is wanted is a standard of comparison that will discriminate among differing degrees of democracy without being prone to sudden mutations; that is sensitive to the difference between genuine stability and counterfeit; and can perhaps take account of some other variables as well. Let us assume that such a dimension of comparability exists and call it "political development." One would then say that *one country is more developed than another if it could be expected to be, normally, more democratic and at the same time more stable,* even though at any given moment it may have departed from its normal position; just as sharp fluctuations of a variable on a graph may nevertheless take place around a clearly visible trend line. The components that enter into calculations of "degree of political development" will then be those underlying characteristics that correlate highly with democracy and constitutional stability but that change only slowly over time.

Let us examine the concept further. Democracy entails general participation in political processes. This certainly means awareness of the national political life, fluency in the national language, and presumably literacy, since the newspaper remains a major device for producing familiarity with the national political process. Newspaper circulation, then, provides one rough index of political development. So does the number enrolled in schools, since literacy and level of information are factors.

Another index that reflects the state of some of the same variables is degree of urbanization—the proportion of the population that lives in cities; for participation, actual or vicarious, in national political life is in Latin America much more an activity of city-dwellers than of people in the countryside. The more people that live in cities, the more that are likely to engage in industrial occupations; so an index of degree of industrialization will be suggestive of the degree of political, as well as that of economic, development.[3]

[3] The appropriate figures for some of the indices mentioned are given in Table I.

Vicarious participation in the common life of the national community is at the same time, of course, the matrix for the complex of feelings known as nationalism, and nationalism is in fact a typical feature of the period of transition from a traditional to a modern way of life.

Although political development is correlated with democracy, this is true only in a general way. That is, a politically developed society may still be transformed into a dictatorship—as the history of twentieth-century Western Europe clearly shows. But dictatorship in a developed society is characteristically different from its counterpart in a traditional society. Traditional dictatorship is content to rule over apathetic and indifferent subjects who merely demonstrate no overt signs of disobedience. Dictatorship in modern societies, on the other hand—those of Hitler, Mussolini, or Perón, for example —aspires, where it reasonably can, to be totalitarian. That is, it starts from the assumption that the citizens will participate in politics. Rather than attempting the impossible, and trying to turn back the clock and impose an indifference to politics, totalitarianism accepts the fact of popular participation, but forces it into channels of support for the regime. One is not forbidden to vote, but compelled to vote—for the single candidate; and lack of inclination to vote or to attend meetings or rallies of the appropriate pro-government organization is interpreted as a sign of opposition to the regime and punished as such.

Political development is normally cumulative and permanent, then, and so serves as a steadier measure of long-term progress than other yardsticks that are susceptible to wide short-term fluctuations.

The creation of a national political community may proceed by many avenues, and a variety of secular changes may show, on examination, development aspects. Land reform—the transfer of the ownership or control of land to those who work it—has all kinds of economic and political meanings, many of which we will deal with below in a different context. But land reform also contributes to political development by conferring responsibility on those who have never borne it before, impelling them, for reasons of economic necessity, to have dealings with the larger world, in whose affairs they must then interest themselves.

THE POLITICAL MEANING OF RACE

It can hardly escape observation that the most highly developed countries of Latin America politically are at the same time among the most European in the ancestry of their population—Uruguay and Costa Rica. The most Indian and African states, on the other hand, are more frequently found toward the lower end of anyone's scale of political development, with either Haiti or Bolivia at the bottom according to any index used—literacy, level of income, newspaper circulation, or any other. Now of course race in a biological sense has nothing to do with this. Today, one surely does not need to point out that no innate biological differences can be presumed to exist that account for social and political differences of this type. The point is rather that "race" in Latin America does denote a certain cultural history and, even today, a distinctive way of life.

The political life of the modern republic in Latin America is, after all, a European invention. Presidents, parliaments, and parties are importations to the New World. Political business is conducted in the European languages, in the cities which were and are the centers of European settlement. To say that over half the population of Guatemala is Indian is to say that a substantial part of the population cannot speak the national language, never reads a newspaper, cannot understand a Presidential speech, does not leave its native districts, and has hardly any contact with national political life. To vary the example: the people of Haiti, the first republic of the 20 present-day Latin American states to gain its independence, are of African descent; the biological fact has no political meaning by itself until one adds the historical gloss that the Haitian people gained sovereignty at virtually the same time as release from slavery; they were illiterate, untutored, and without civic skills or the means of developing them. This is the political meaning of "race" and statistics on race as they relate to progress in political development.

When the Spaniards came, they found three major Indian civili-

zations in the New World where large sedentary bodies of population lived at an advanced stage of cultural evolution, the Aztec, the
Maya, and the Inca. The successor states of these indigenous empires are today the countries with the largest numbers of unassimi-
lated Indian inhabitants—Mexico, Guatemala, Ecuador, Peru, and
Bolivia, reading from north to south.

One assumes that, sooner or later, genuine social transformations
—that is, revolutions in the real sense—will take place that will bring
about the full participation of the indigenous inhabitants in the
political life of their countries. The successful Independence movements were not of this character. They were civil conflicts among
the Europeans, with the Spaniards born in the New World, the
creoles, winning their freedom from Spaniards originating in the
Iberian peninsula itself, the *peninsulares*. Even in Mexico, where the
Independence movement had had roots in the Indian population,
it was soon taken over by the creole upper classes.

Genuine social overturns having as consequence the admission of
Indians to the national community are taking place in Mexico, beginning with the Revolution of 1910, and in Bolivia, dating from
the Revolution of 1952. A revolutionary process in Guatemala that
might have ended with similar results was cut short in 1954 with
the overthrow of the Arbenz Guzmán government, and the *status
quo ante* restored. Ecuador and Peru remain leading candidates for
social revolution, accordingly, as Guatemala does for a renewal of
hers.

The admission of Indians to the national political community does
not mean necessarily that they occupy positions of political leadership *as Indians*. If the example of Mexico, the state furthest along
in this process, is typical, it is the *mestizo,* the person of mixed
ancestry, who dominates politics at the expense of both European
and Indian. As the Indian is progressively assimilated into the
national community, rather, he loses his character as Indian, and
becomes simply another Mexican. For example, in the conservative
Mexico City daily newspaper, *Excelsior,* news of the Indian predominates on the first page of the second section—in the news of

TABLE I *Some Social Characteristics of the Latin American States*

	Daily News-paper Circulation (per thousand)	Estimated Real 1961 Gross National Product ($ per capita)	Literacy (per cent)	Ancestry
Argentina	180	799.0	97	Predominantly European
Uruguay	180	560.9	97	Predominantly European
Cuba	129	516.0	60	Mainly European, many African and mulatto
Panama	124	371.0	72	Mainly mestizo and mulatto, some European
Costa Rica	102	361.6	79	Predominantly European
Venezuela	102	644.5	42	Mainly mestizo, some mulatto
Nicaragua	90	288.4	57	Mainly mestizo
Peru	76	268.5	50	Mainly Indian, many mestizo and European
Chile	74*	452.9	80	Mainly mestizo, many European
Brazil	63	374.6	43	Mainly European, many African and mulatto
Colombia	59	373.4	63	Mainly mestizo, many European
Ecuador	50*	222.7	56	Mainly Indian and mestizo, some European
Mexico	48*	415.4	57	Mainly mestizo, many Indian, some European
El Salvador	43	267.5	45	Mainly mestizo
Bolivia	34	122.3	42	Mainly Indian and mestizo
Dominican Republic	29	313.2	43	Mainly mulatto and European
Paraguay	28	193.2	—	Predominantly mestizo

TABLE I *Continued*

	Daily News-paper Circu-lation (per thousand)	Estimated Real 1961 Gross Na-tional Product ($ per capita)	Literacy (per cent)	Ancestry
Honduras	25	251.7	37	Predominantly mestizo
Guatemala	22	257.7	28	Mainly Indian and mestizo
Haiti	3	149.2	11	Predominantly African

NOTE: Data on newspaper circulation for 1956-58, except those with asterisk, which date from 1952.

Sources: 1) Newspaper circulation, *UN Statistical Yearbook, 1960.*
2) National product, P. N. Rosenstein-Rodan, "International Aid for Underdeveloped Countries," *The Review of Economics and Statistics,* May, 1961.
3) Literacy, Harold E. Davis, ed., *Government and Politics in Latin America, Ronald,* New York, 1958, except that the figure given for Uruguay is the author's estimate; the figure for Paraguay is omitted as palpably unreliable.
4) Ancestry, author's estimates.

crimes of violence. News of the Mexican of Spanish descent is found in abundance on page one, section three—the society columns. Page one of section one—the news of national politics—tells of the doings of the *mestizo.*

C. ISSUES IN THE EVOLUTION OF LATIN AMERICAN POLITICS

At any one time there will be a political issue, or an interrelated set of issues, which structure national politics. As conditions change, as new problems arise, as old problems are resolved or become obsolete, the central issue of yesterday's politics is replaced by another that serves in its turn as the orientation point of political activity. The parties measure off their positions to the left and right of the central axis; if the old parties refuse to adapt, new parties arise with programs focussing on the new set of issues.

It may be, as Seymour Martin Lipset has argued, that one of the key determinants of the structure of a party system and of the style of political conflict will be whether a polity solves its problems as they arise, clearing the slate to proceed to the next major problem, or whether it allows the divisions occasioned by problems of former years to continue, perpetuating the hostilities and party divisions of precious decades and even centuries, and thereby marring the functioning of the political process. Much evidence tending to substantiate this thesis can be found in the history of the Latin American republics.

It is possible without doing major violence to the facts to generalize as follows about the succession of issues that the political systems of Hispanic America have faced.

THE INDEPENDENCE PERIOD

During the first half-century of Independence, the problems faced immediately were those that concerned the basic organization of the new states: constitutional questions of centralism *versus* federalism, the right of secession, the form of the government, and the powers of the Chief Executive and how he should be chosen. To be sure, questions of this type occasionally appear even today; but a century and a quarter ago they were the major issues to be faced. Then the party struggle was Centralist *versus* Federalist,[4] or, as the parties usually adopted the nomenclature then general, Conservative *versus* Liberal.[5] Often, to be sure, the struggle would be based on personal ambitions rather than on questions of principle, and even when questions of principle were primary, personal ambition would not be far behind (as of course it never is, in party politics). Party combat was at the time, on the whole, physical combat, for several rea-

[4] Outside the United States, a "federalist" is invariably what we would call a states' righter.
[5] In Argentina the Conservatives were federalist. Elsewhere they favored strong central authority, as in the early United States.

sons. In the first place, Independence had been won by warfare, and the leaders of the new states were generals who naturally turned to force as the arbiter of disputes. In any case, no peaceful procedures for solving disputes existed—the disputes themselves were precisely over the machinery of government that should be constructed; to accept a mode of settling disputes peacefully would already be a settlement of the substance of the disputes themselves. How could a secessionist accept the decision of a *national* tribunal? Why should the believer in a strong executive, elected for a life term, a sort of republican monarch, debate the merits of his case in a legislature he believed should never have been called?

Eventually, the basic issues at stake here were settled, usually by violence, more or less definitively. The general outlines of the constitutional systems operating today were already visible 100 years ago. National boundaries were at last settled in most places, although Cuba and Panama only became independent in 1902 and 1903, respectively. Boundary disputes continue to exist, of course, but they are between established states whose existence itself would not be placed in jeopardy by the adverse settlement of the territorial issue in question.

During the initial period after Independence, however, issues of actual national existence were basic ones. The countries of Central America constituted a single federation from 1823 to 1839. For part of the same period, Colombia, Venezuela, and Ecuador constituted a federation under the name *Gran Colombia*. Argentina did not acknowledge the independence of Uruguay until 1851 and had initially attempted to include Paraguay within her borders.

THE RADICAL PERIOD

The themes of Latin American politics in the second half-century of Independence were of a different character. One might call the years 1860-1925—very roughly speaking—the "Radical period"; the issues that dominated politics were those that figured in the platforms of the Radical parties founded at the time. In some countries, such as Argentina or Chile, separate Radical parties were founded;

in others, such as Uruguay or Colombia, the Radicals simply formed one tendency among partisans of Liberalism.

Radicalism meant, in the first place, laicism—that is, opposition to any role for religion in the life of the state.[6] This anti-clericalism, as it is usually called, had always been one of the basic principles of nineteenth-century Liberalism, but was stressed more heavily by the Radicals. Radicalism also meant political reform, perhaps complete constitutional overhaul, but certainly reform in election procedures. It might also mean the beginnings of labor and social legislation— but only the beginnings, for the Radicals were not workingmen by and large, but professional people: lawyers, schoolteachers, and journalists typically, though with a sprinkling of "enlightened" businessmen and skilled workers.

Let us consider the points in the Radical program one by one. Anti-clericalism is a policy not generally understood by North Americans, accustomed to the separation of the two kingdoms and unfamiliar with religious intervention in politics. Anti-clericalism opposes the Church on various grounds, the importance of each varying somewhat in accordance with local circumstances. The Church's role in educating the young is always abhorrent to the Radical intellectual who regards it as imposing a bondage on the mind of the young contrary to liberal principles. At the same time, he may object to the Church's possession of extensive lands—in some countries they constituted up to a third, or even more, of the arable area—as an impediment to economic progress; whereas the Church's exemption from taxes he believes throws a heavier burden on the more productive segments of the population. That is, economic and ideological motives may mingle, as they will do, to form a middle-class anti-clericalism of businessmen, teachers, and journalists; those concerned with economic as well as intellectual freedom. Accordingly, it was the usual pattern (though not in Argentina) for Radical or Radical-Liberal governments at least to separate Church and

---

[6] In Peru, the Radical movement stressed instead the elimination of military intervention from politics, and the party became known as the *Partido Civilista*. Anti-clericalism did not become a major issue in Peru.

State, for example, as Alessandri did in Chile, or even to confiscate Church property, as Juárez did in Mexico. The Radicals also objected to religious monopolization of the rites that signal the major events of the life-cycle, and they supported civil marriage and burial, the civil registration of births, and the permission of divorce.

Progressive leaders of the Radical period were also very much concerned with electoral and constitutional reform. Batlle y Ordóñez in Uruguay and Alessandri in Chile were particularly strong advocates of constitutional change, and each was responsible for his country's getting a new constitution, Uruguay's being adopted in 1919 and Chile's in 1925.

The Radicals were interested in electoral reform not only for ideological reasons, to be sure, but also because, since they enjoyed greater popular support than did the conservative and landowning classes, they could expect electoral success proportionate to the representative quality of the elections. The Conservatives, on the other hand, suspected the same thing, and regularly kept themselves in power by manipulation of the election machinery and restriction of the suffrage. The Argentine Radical Civic Union had made honest elections one of the central points in its program from its founding in 1890, for example, while the slogan of Mexican liberalism at the ouster of Porfirio Díaz after 35 years of rule in 1910 was the same as it had been at his accession: "effective suffrage—no reelection."

The Radical movement did not run its full course in all the countries of Latin America; in most of them, for a substantial part of the "Radical period," political development was interrupted by dictatorship and free political activity was interdicted. Where politics was free, however, the central issues were those that Radicalism had made its own.

Of course, this was the Radical period in all the independent states of the West, and there is a strong family resemblance among all the Radical and Radical-Liberal movements that flourished at this time, and indeed among their typical leaders: the popular hero, ex-journalist, -professor, or -businessman, with a dynamic personality and a touch of demagoguery and dictatorialness, liberal and ideal-istic but careful to stop well short of socialism. Irigoyen in Argen-tina, Alessandri in Chile, were surely cut from the same cloth as Clemenceau, Lloyd George, and Woodrow Wilson. Batlle y Ordóñez deviated from the general pattern somewhat in lacking the dicta-torial personality and in being prepared to go further to the Left in his social policies.

THE RECONSTRUCTION PERIOD

In 1922, Mussolini's Fascist movement took over the government of Italy. In 1924, a young Peruvian intellectual named Haya de la Torre founded APRA, the American Popular Revolutionary Alli-ance, a movement of the democratic Left. The key problem of the succeeding years was to be the alleviation of the economic misery, sharpened by the worldwide Great Depression, which gave fascism its opportunity, and the democratic Left its leading task. The pro-grams written in these years were blueprints for the uplifting of the down-trodden; most of the new parties founded were either fascist or social liberal of the APRA type. Indeed it seemed at times as if some of them tried to be both, like the National Revolutionary Movement (MNR) of Bolivia.

Many of the old-style dictators of the area took on fascist trappings and fashioned some home-made fascist ideology to try to become identified with what the misguided of the time thought was "the wave of the future"; Getúlio Vargas in Brazil, for example. But this was no more than a case of keeping up with the fashions, and when the styles changed the outmoded clothes were put away. In some countries—Mexico, Chile, Brazil, Ecuador, Bolivia—new movements genuinely fascist, in doctrine, uniforms, and style of political action, were founded; but these never became serious contenders for power. Only in Argentina, with Peronism, was there a movement authen-tically owing anything to fascism that had a lasting impact.

Parties similar in orientation to the APRA, on the other hand, which were founded during this period, have come to play the dominant role in Mexico, Venezuela, and Costa Rica, as well as in

Bolivia and in Peru itself. In addition, countries without a dominant party of the APRA type have had *aprista*-like Presidents who have inaugurated "New Deal" programs.

Of course, this was the period of the world struggle against fascism, culminating in World War II, which had an indirect but powerful influence on Latin America itself. Economically, the war years were years of economic boom in Latin America, as the United States turned increasingly to countries of the area to supply raw materials for the war effort, many former sources of which were then under Axis control. At the same time, prices for the peacetime export products of the area were abnormally high, due to their relative scarcity under wartime conditions. Furthermore, the unavailability of many manufactured products formerly procured from the United States and Britain gave an impetus to the development of local industry, especially in the larger countries of the area, which had a sizeable domestic market.

The central issues of the period 1925-50 were thus those stemming from economic reconstruction, on the one hand—over social security, labor organization, and government regulation of the economy —and, on the other hand, those over international diplomatic and ideological alignment.

THE CURRENT PHASE

Since about 1950 the themes of Latin American politics have been different enough from those of the years immediately preceding that one can profitably speak of a new period in the politics of the area. That is, while the processes of politics have not necessarily changed, the central issues are significantly different from those of the immediate past to the extent that the period merits separate treatment.

The focal issues of the last decade, and surely of the two or three decades to come, are those centering on the problems of economic development and of the cold war. The two issues have many points of intersection with each other, but are, of course, analytically quite separate.

In a general way, one can say that there has always been a concern for economic development, and the period of 20 years or so before the end of the nineteenth century, especially, saw a variety of government actions motivated by this concern. Today, however, economic development policy is clearly the central issue above all others. This phenomenon is not confined to Latin America, but is quite general in today's world; it comes about for several reasons.

In the first place, the tremendous rise in the rate of population growth must be held a contributory factor. Given the steady increase in population, merely to maintain the current *per capita* level of life needs a substantial expansion of employment opportunities and of national production. While the increase in the rate of population growth is taking place today generally all over the globe, it is especially marked in Latin America where, for example, the birthrate in Guatemala is currently the second highest national birthrate in the world, according to the figures available, and about twice that of the United States.

Latin America, too, has shared in what has come to be known as "the revolution of rising expectations"—that is, the new and growing conviction among the less-favored peoples that it is not inevitable that one live at a bare subsistence level, eking out a precarious and miserable life amid squalor and disease. To some extent, modern communications techniques have contributed to this phenomenon by acquainting the peoples of the southern half of the globe with the manner of living in the developed societies. The extensive mobility of Europeans and North Americans has had a similar effect. In some cases, there was also the influence of returning veterans who had themselves witnessed the wonders of the modern world in the course of their travels, or had at least acquired a restlessness and an impatience with the old ways.[7]

Concomitant with the revolution of rising expectations, and itself

[7] Mexico, Brazil, and Colombia have sent expeditionary forces to fight alongside those of the United States in one or another of the wars of the twentieth century. Bolivia and Paraguay fought the bloody Chaco War in the 1930s, while several other states have fought over border questions.

providing a stimulant to it, is the fact that in the present international environment, the chances that foreign aid will be available to assist a development program are very good indeed. Two related factors are of importance here: the Cold War and the existence of the United Nations organization.

The Cold War means several things in this connection. It means that one or both of the superpowers may be ready to assist in a development program as a way of attempting to insure against hostile acts on the part of a small state. It means that the general stalemate between the superpowers enables the small state to pursue a line of policy independent of big-Power domination, each major Power being reluctant to use extreme measures of coercion for fear that they may lead to general war, or at least to a local installment of such a war; or that they may drive the small state and its sympathizers into an alliance with the main adversary. It may also be possible for a small state to ally itself with one of the major Powers and extract substantial amounts of aid by raising the specter that without aid revolution may come, with the consequent formation of a hostile government; or by urging the advantages of aid to create a "showcase" of the beneficial effects of the social system that the small state allegedly shares with its big-Power patron.

The existence of the United Nations General Assembly, in which each small state has a voice and a vote, and thus the partial ability to inflict "propaganda defeats," gives the small state's plea for aid in its development program a certain weight it might not have otherwise. At the same time, the specialized organs of the United Nations can themselves provide modest technical assistance that will be less subject to the charge that it constitutes foreign intervention than assistance which bears the character of aid from one state to another.

The institution of an economic development program entails normally the adoption of several types of government policy; central planning and state investment, with concomitant controls on economic activity of various types, together with revision of the tax structure; the encouragement of foreign investment, private or public, or both; a policy of stabilization of the value of the currency, likely otherwise to become inflated as the development program generates new purchasing power without producing new consumers' goods in its early stages; and perhaps changes in the organization of the agricultural sector.

The problems of economic development policy will be surveyed in detail in a subsequent section. But clearly, an economic development program will provide plenty of issues for political controversy. The lines of division that such issues impose on the politically active population may well be related to the lines that form over Cold War questions. With the creation, with the later developments in the Cuban Revolution, of a government in the Americas that leans East in the Cold War, Cold War issues have taken on relevance for inter-American relations. That is, one's attitude toward the present government of Cuba has become itself a pseudo-Cold War issue, and makes of immediate concern other issues of the Cold War proper, which would surely otherwise not have intruded themselves into the domestic politics of the Latin American republics with such force.

Over these questions in current controversy, as over the key issues of other periods, new parties are in process of forming. Pro-Castro and pro-Soviet parties, which attract more supporters than do the Communists themselves—"popular socialist" parties, as some of them are called [8]—have been formed. Pre-existing parties at a loss for an issue—the Republican Democratic Union in Venezuela is an example—have taken up Fidel Castro's cause, and found new popular support.

At the same time, the Cuban and other Cold War-related issues have had an impact on the established parties; fissures have developed within the *aprista* parties, most notably, with the parties' leadership taking the anti-Castro position. In several countries, at

---

[8] The designation "National Liberation Movement" or "Front of National Liberation" is also common; the Costa Rican Party of National Liberation, one should note, however, antedates this use of the term, and is *aprista* and not pro-Soviet.

the time of writing, the split has been taken to the point of the secession of the party's left wing and its conversion into a "popular
socialist" type of party.

This concludes our brief survey of the development of the key
issues of Latin American politics, and of the parties that grew out
of the conflicts described. While many of the issues discussed
achieved some kind of definitive settlement, others did not, and continue to exist today in modified or attenuated form, like the Church-
State controversy in some countries. The parties that developed out
of specific positions on the issues of the day in some cases disappeared together with the issues that gave them birth; in some cases
they continue to exist, trying to keep alive issues of little relevance
to new national problems; in yet other cases they have found new
issues on which to appeal for popular support; while sometimes of
course the party continues in existence without real issues, as a
simple alliance of assorted politicians for electoral purposes. What
type of fate awaited the different parties depended in part on the
political, and especially the electoral, environment in which they
operated. This, together with the position of the parties today, will
be considered in a subsequent section.

II   *Political Processes*

A. PERSPECTIVE

EXPLAINING LATIN AMERICAN POLITICS

How does one go about *explaining* why Latin American politics takes the forms it does? There are no problems in *describing* the major features of politics in the area: the central role of the military, the prevalence of violence, the ascendancy of dominant personalities rather than the sway of impersonally functioning institutions, the widespread graft and nepotism—these are the commonplaces of commentary. There are commonplaces of interpretation, too, but their power of explanation no longer compels, if it ever did. Latin American authors themselves have traditionally been free with "racial" explanations that cite alleged deficiencies in the Indian races, or in peoples of mixed blood; these are largely out of fashion now, even in Latin America. Economic and cultural explanations, on the other hand, are still popular: the gulf separating social classes, poverty, illiteracy, lead to a politics of desperation and violence, one reads; alternatively, the colonial past, or the heritage of the Iberian peninsula itself, can be shown to have set the patterns of authoritarian rule that persist today.

Explanations along these lines, however, while plausible enough so long as one considers only the American republics themselves, lose their force when one tries to apply them on a wider scale. Poverty and illiteracy have after all been the rule in human societies, in the stable and orderly ones, too; while on the other hand a politics of violence, a "Latin American" type of politics, is becoming visible in countries that have never known Spanish or Portuguese rule.

33

Consider for a moment recent events in the former Belgian Congo: independence from the colonial Power is followed by a struggle between federalists and centralists; a charismatic *caudillo,* Patrice Lumumba, is captured by his rivals and, predictably, the *ley fuga* is applied in the classic Latin American manner—he is shot "while trying to escape."

The reasons for the existence of the major features of Latin American political dynamics become clearer if one takes a rather different perspective, one that places at the forefront of the inquiry the fact that the stability of a system of political institutions rests on an acceptance of those institutions as legitimate.

In a stable polity, that is, the maintenance of order does not rest routinely on the application of force. Force is kept in reserve, of course, to put down the occasional violations of the peace; but normally political life moves in well-marked channels, in accordance with pre-adjusted patterns of behavior. This is, surely, true by definition since this is what we have in mind in speaking of a stable political system. Now in the short run, in an immediate sense, observance of the rules of the game, willingness to stay within the marked channels, is a matter of habit. One does what is customary; one follows precedent. In the long run, however, when out-of-the-ordinary circumstances arise, when methods of handling new situations must be devised—that is, when new institutional patterns of behavior are to be created—then existent patterns are reproduced, or new patterns are created, because they conform to accepted ideas of legitimacy. These ideas will be peculiar to the time, and perhaps to the place; nevertheless, they will be accepted as natural and right. For example: a group of North Americans organized in a club or society are faced with the necessity of making some collective decision. They take a vote, and the majority preference becomes the group decision. Perfectly natural to us; yet strange and repugnant to Samoans, who, we are told, allot decision-making power only to heads of extended families; or to traditionalist Indonesians, who prefer to talk things out until a consensus is reached; or even to our own ancestors of four centuries ago.

To carry the reasoning a step further: one obeys a person in authority because he has come by his office in the proper manner; in a manner which is established by precedent, of course, but which also is "right" in being based on accepted principles of legitimacy.[1] From this point of view, the features of political life traditionally characteristic of Latin America derive from the existence of what might be called a "legitimacy vacuum." The Latin American states are passing through a period of transition between one set of principles of legitimacy and another; during the period of transition some features have survived from the old way, some have developed as precursors of the new, but for the most part legitimacy does not attach to existent institutions. In the absence of stable patterns of legitimate political behavior, no alternatives exist to the dominance of personality, the absence of public spirit, and the rule of force.

LEGITIMACY IN THE COLONIES AND TODAY

The central feature of the colonial legitimacy system in Latin America was that political power, like social status, depended on the acknowledgement of the rights of birth. This was clearly true at the very top rank of the political order: the monarch came into his title by inheritance. The legitimacy of the tenure of office of inferior authorities, in turn, rested on royal appointment, and so the whole structure of authority derived legitimacy from this inherited title. But social status conferred by birth constituted the normal prerequisite for the holding of high office in any case; moreover, the leading offices in the Spanish colonies were reserved for Spaniards born in the peninsula itself, rather than in the New World, throughout virtually the whole of the colonial period. The scope of one's political functions, then, was defined by the rank into which one was born.

[1] Whether one obeys or not will probably also depend on whether the injunction is a lawful one, that is, on whether the official is acting in the way he is supposed, on whether he is staying within the bounds of our expectations as to his behavior. For present purposes, however, I wish to stress the idea of legitimacy especially as it applies to the right to hold an office, rather than to the behavior imputed to the office.

The nature of the role ascribed to the holder of public office reflected this situation. The duties of upper officials were unspecialized, and did not require tedious training or the acquisition of skills unbecoming to a gentleman. At the top of the local colonial hierarchy, administrative roles were actually not even differentiated into separate political, military, and religious categories, the colonial governor being responsible for saving souls and leading military campaigns as much as for collecting taxes and keeping the roads in repair. The minimal technical skills that were necessary were regularly provided by the clergy, who formed an integral part of the governing system.

Authority in this system, then, came from the top down, deriving from the rights of birth, and ultimately from God's grace. To be sure, there were occasional ambiguities over the details of the rules governing the precedence of different degrees of relationship in inheriting a throne, and there were, accordingly, succession crises. Nevertheless, normally the inheritability of the position of supreme authority, like the criteria of status based on birth that applied to eligibility for lesser positions, made possible stability and continuity in the political order.

Today, no one is "born to rule" in any place that is touched by the modern spirit. In modern political systems, supreme authority can be derived legitimately only from popular choice. Legitimacy comes now not from "above" but from "below."

A whole series of lesser principles flows from this revolution in basic political values. Popular sovereignty presupposes and reinforces juridical equality and equality of social opportunity. Given equality of opportunity, the criterion of public personnel policy becomes merit, not social status; while in a public service based on merit, technical specialization becomes possible (as it cannot be in a service based on class), high standards of technical proficiency can be expected, and government can take on increasingly complex functions.

If popular sovereignty thus makes the welfare state possible, it also makes it probable—following the ancient Aristotelian maxim, rediscovered by Harrington and again by Hamilton, that the distribution of property tends to follow the distribution of power. That is, a democracy is likely to redistribute property in the direction of equality (through a system of progressive taxation that supports social services benefiting especially the poorer citizens, etc.).

One is thus likely to find the institutions of the modern polity accepted as legitimate not only because of the habitual acceptance commanded by any stably operating political order, but also because governments functioning within it—for electoral purposes, if for no other—clearly attempt to govern in the interest of as wide a segment of the population as possible; because of the general conformity of official administrative actions to rational technical criteria; and because the popular will is obviously the highest authority in the state.

THE "LEGITIMACY VACUUM"

With the fairly clear exception of Uruguay, none of the Latin American republics has emerged altogether into the modern period in its political and social institutions. Some occupy a position not far from the pole of the colonial polity; others are clearly in steady progress toward the modern pole; and all combine some features of old and new, together with key characteristics of the process of transition itself.

What has happened, in effect, is that the Wars of Independence succeeded in sweeping away the colonial system, in eliminating any possibility of relying on the idea that legitimate authority comes from above, from the royal succession sanctioned by the grace of God, without replacing it by a system of practice based on the belief that legitimate authority comes from below, from the popular will. Contrast the American and French Revolutions, which had ended royal authority to replace it with new conceptions of political right, conceptions that impelled a reordering of social institutions on the basis of the principle of equality. After abortive attempts in Mexico and Haiti, and a successful attempt in Brazil, at establishing indigenous dynasties, the newly independent republics became, regardless of what their constitutions said, turbulent oligarchies, in which the possession of power lacked that overwhelming legitimation that comes from its being derived from a great principle of right. The locus of power at a given moment, accordingly, was regarded as arbitrary and could be contested by whoever was able.

However, the constitution itself was nominally based upon the notion of popular sovereignty and embellished with mottoes taken from the French and American Revolutions. But the social reality, and operative social beliefs, were so strongly at variance with the doctrines expressed in the constitution, that the document necessarily failed to provide an actual working guide for the political system. To this day, of course—to the surprise of North Americans—the Latin American constitution tends rather to be regarded as a statement of ideals, a set of aspirations, rather than a sober directive to which political reality must conform.

Politics existed then and, for the most part, exist today in a "legitimacy vacuum." In the absence of any compelling legitimation of the right to hold office of the present incumbents, in many states their term lasts as long as they can maintain themselves by force of arms. In the absence of a set of operative ideals that inform the behavior patterns of everyday political life, cynicism predominates, public office is used to promote private advantage, and nepotism and theft become cardinal principles of public administration. If the chief criterion of public personnel selection under the Crown was birth, and in a democracy is merit, then in a legitimacy vacuum it is personal loyalty. Because one's hold on power is so insecure, to remain in power becomes the all-important objective. One dare not take chances, in such a situation, by relying on strangers; positions of trust must necessarily be given to fellow-partisans and, where possible, to relatives.

Where institutions carry no conviction, and where the bonds of party are too often only those of self-interest, the single available alternative focus of loyalty and faith is the individual leader: and personalism is of one piece with the lack of public spirit and the absence of a doctrine of legitimacy. Militarism, too, is an unavoidable concomitant. Where authority is not respected, force must be resorted to. Where force is used, the army necessarily has the last word. In this type of situation, the army is in politics whether it wants to be or not.

Looked at in this light, those distinctive features of Latin American politics that have been explained racially or culturally or economically can be seen rather to be attributes of a certain stage of political evolution, a time of transition, the period of a legitimacy vacuum. Accordingly, they can be found elsewhere, wherever polities must pass from a set of institutions based on one principle to another set resting on a different premise. One can find a "Latin American politics" in Europe in the age of the transition from the hierarchy of reciprocal obligation of the late Middle Ages to the monarchical sovereignty of the early modern period; or in Rome during the transition from republic to empire.

If this thesis has a meaning for the present time, it is that Latin American politics, in the present era, cannot become stable and peaceful, unless it is re-structured on the basis of the only contemporarily available conception of legitimacy—which is, today even more than a century and a half ago, popular sovereignty and juridical and social equality. When this is accepted as the basis of institutions and policy, a breakthrough into a new world of legitimacy is achieved. This was, at bottom, the nature of the change wrought by Batlle in Uruguay and begun by Carranza and Obregón in Mexico; in both countries, political stability came as a consequence of the development of a policy of social and economic progress for all sectors of the population within a democratic framework.

Often, in superficial analyses, the requirements of stability and those of democracy and social equality are opposed to each other. But, today, the stability achieved at the expense of democratic ideals can only be an optical illusion; it lives by force and will die by force. The basis for a stability that abides can today only be a foundation of democratic legitimacy, achieved by the institution of a regime which, in the process of policy-making and in the substance of policy itself, is responsive to the popular will. We shall return to this theme in the concluding section of this book.

B. THE PRESS AND PUBLIC OPINION

THE PRESS

Before discussing the character and political role of the Latin American newspaper, one should make clear that the term "the press" embraces a broad range of periodicals of widely varying quality, views, and political impact. The difficulty inherent in arriving at any fair over-all picture may be in part responsible for the dearth of any literature on the political role of the press in Latin America, despite its palpable importance.

One indication of the key role the newspapers play in shaping public opinion, if any were needed, can be found in the political importance of the newspaper publisher himself in Latin America. Examples come to mind such as Laureano Gómez, who has dominated Conservative politics in Colombia for 30 years; Pedro Beltrán, recently Prime Minister of Peru; or Harmodo Arias, whose control of a large portion of the Panamanian press helps to make him one of the three or four most important men in the country.

Although the range in quality of the newspapers of Latin America is great, one would probably be justified in saying that the over-all average, in terms of journalistic standards of objectivity of reporting and breadth of coverage, is low. Partisan bias and sensationalist handling of the news might be expected in the mass-circulation tabloids; it certainly occurs at that level in the United States, and in England too, despite the superb quality of the leading English newspapers. But one finds less-than-objective handling of news stories even in the respectable press—even *El Tiempo* of Bogotá, for example, which enjoys an international reputation, is not immune; while the deliberate distortion of the news one finds in *El Comercio* of Lima, the leading Peruvian newspaper, reaches astonishing proportions.

This feature of the Latin American press, the deliberate distortion of the news, is presumably due to the more emotional and more extreme character of partisanship in Latin American politics. An inadvertent lowering of quality derives, in addition, from the usual situation of poor communications in the country and the lack of integration of the various regions which means that often the press of the capital has only the vaguest notion of what is going on in the remoter areas. The author has read a news story in a Lima paper about a series of events in the interior for which the source was a dispatch appearing in a Paris newspaper! The counterpart to this is that often the newspaper's circulation is confined to the cities and hardly reaches the interior. One may be tempted, accordingly, to sympathize with the complaints about the press frequently made by Latin American governments.

Nevertheless the extent of government regulation of the press seems excessive to the North American. The network of official regulations, many dating from colonial days, have as their ostensible aim the avoidance of immorality, defamation of character, and sedition. Clearly, such regulations are susceptible of abuse by governments desiring to limit the freedom of the press to be critical.

But there are many other ways in which government influence can be brought to bear on the press, and opposition journals made to feel the consequences of incurring official disfavor. Some of the devices that have actually been used in the Latin American states include the following, taken from the recent history of Argentina, Honduras, and El Salvador. The press may be required to print all government news releases, without comment, thereby being forced to surrender the bulk of its columns to official propaganda. Licenses to publish, or to practice the profession of a journalist, may be required, and may be withheld from unsuitable applicants. The government may monopolize the supply of newsprint, setting quotas a paper is to receive in terms of how compliant it is with government wishes. If newsprint must come from abroad, a similar purpose can be achieved by controlling the foreign exchange available to papers with which to buy it. The favorable rates at which public services—cable, telephone, mail—are provided to the press may be withheld from certain periodicals on a variety of pretexts. Applicable tax or minimum wage rates may be adjusted upwards. And so on.

Although outright censorship is often employed, governments prefer to avoid this if possible because of the sensitivity to the issue of freedom of the press in Latin America. In addition, a Freedom of the Press committee of the Inter-American Press Association exists, which makes a practice of drawing attention throughout the hemisphere to denials of press freedom.

PUBLIC OPINION

From what has already been written on social structure, it is possible to surmise much of the structure of public opinion. That is, in most of Latin America normally effective national public opinion is limited to the urban areas, and indeed confined for most purposes to upper-status groups. In recent years the leadership of organized labor has entered the circle of those whose opinions can be brought to bear on the policy-making process without resort to violence. On some occasions, in important elections or in revolutions, public opinion among the more quiescent areas of society can be mobilized, but this is not the normal day-to-day situation.

The divisions of public opinion follow class lines, social class being a more definite, more pervasive, and more important thing in Latin America than in the United States. They also follow party lines, the leadership being given by the party spokesmen and press.

The major single influence on the formation of political opinion in each country, however, is that of the government leadership, whose doings and especially whose pronouncements take up a much larger proportion of newspaper columns than is customary in the United States.

The second major influence on the formation of public opinion in Latin America is the Catholic Church. The influence of the Church hierarchy extends beyond questions of the relations of Church and State and may on occasion be brought to bear on the whole range of national political problems. Historically, this influence was exercised on behalf of the forces of order and the *status quo*. Those in authority are placed there by God; the troubles we experience in this world try us and prepare us for the next; to rebel against constituted authority because it does not alleviate, or worsens, adverse conditions is thus sinful; and so on.

Clerical influence is especially strong among the rural people, for whom the priest is likely to be the most educated man with whom they come into contact, and at the same time someone whose functions are a vital part of their daily lives. Clerical influence in the cities, especially among women, should not be underestimated, however.

The Church's identification with the forces of order was never absolute, though, and there have been signs in recent years of an acknowledgement of the grievances of peasants and workers as legitimate, and an acceptance of organization and political action as means for their remedy. Catholic trade unions have been a feature of the labor world for nearly half a century now, although they have had a substantial membership only since World War II.

In addition, as was mentioned above, the Church has in recent years been forced through experience to realize that eventually support of a modern dictator or even passive failure to oppose him involves it in self-abasement and acquiescence in plainly immoral practices; but one may be pardoned for reserving judgment on the question of how well the lesson has been learned. The Church broke with Perón, and later, with Trujillo, only after it had been directly attacked following mild protests at being pushed beyond all tolerable limits. The record of the Church in Colombia with respect to the rule of Rojas Pinilla is better; in the case of the present Paraguayan dictatorship, the most favorable judgment is that the Church hierarchy's position has been ambiguous, although individual priests have made clear their opposition to the regime.

There is currently in progress a resurgence of clerical activity in politics, even in Mexico, where the Church had recently been pursuing a policy of caution and non-involvement. The occasion for this is the promotion of a strong anti-Communist offensive, prompted by the favorable attitude toward Communism and the Soviet bloc shown by Fidel Castro, and designed to counteract incursions of *fidelismo* in other states of the Americas.

Fidelismo itself forms one of the currents of popular opinion to-day, based largely on long-standing anti-Americanism on the Left. To a large extent, being pro-Fidel Castro today is simply the current way of being anti-American, in that Fidel has defied the Yankees and has thus far "gotten away" with it. It is more, and less, than that, however; it is also one of the current forms that youthful idealism takes, and is most marked among the youth, especially in the universities.

The anti-Americanism that exists is perhaps only what could be expected of countries that find themselves in juxtaposition to a colossus whose every act affects them vitally, and might ruin them, while he is hardly aware of their existence. Porfirio Díaz has been quoted as having said "Poor Mexico! So far from God, and so close to the United States." That this overwhelming proximity is the key factor here is strongly suggested by the fact that precisely the same type of anti-Americanism can be encountered widely in Canada.[2]

Anti-Americanism on cultural grounds, with the theme that North Americans are cultural barbarians, is found especially among the intellectuals, of course. Marxism—in its cruder forms—is met with, too, also principally among the intellectuals, although some simpli-fied versions have filtered down to elements of the politically con-scious working classes. From a Marxist or pseudo-Marxist viewpoint, the United States is objectionable as the leading capitalist state, of course; and Marxist views—especially Lenin's theory of imperialism as a stage of capitalism—can be made to dovetail fairly neatly with traditional Latin American anti-Yankeeism, though it would still be a mistake, and quite misleading, to confound the two.

Public opinion is also structured by region. Regionalism is strong within most Latin American countries; natural barriers to com-munication, especially the great mountain ranges, segment nations into self-conscious regions. Very often regional differences are

---

[2] A Canadian statesman has remarked that Canada ought to begin a techni-cal assistance program to the African and Asian countries to teach them anti-Americanism, seeing that Canada is the oldest and most experienced practi-tioner of the art.

accentuated by ethnic differences going back before Columbus; between the Quechua- and Aymará-speaking areas of Bolivia, for example, hostile feelings are traditional.

A common situation is for inter-regional tension to be dominated by an overriding rivalry between the two leading cities, or between city and hinterland.[3] Inter-city rivalry is strong in Brazil (between Rio de Janeiro and São Paulo), in Colombia (between Bogotá, Cali, and Medellín), in Ecuador (between Quito and Guayaquil), and is incipient in Mexico (between Mexico City and Monterrey). The second city has grown because it is favorably located for industrial or commercial development, as a rule, and is more business-minded, and indeed business-like, than the capital. Thus, the bustling *Paulista,* or the hardworking *Antioqueño* (from Medellín), complains of the laziness and inefficiency of the people in the capital, inert and enmeshed in red tape, and not pulling their weight in the common effort.[4] There is business activity in the capital, of course— in fact Mexico recently embarked on a program to try to get industry started outside the Federal District, where it is concentrated—but a larger proportion of it is in commercial, banking, insurance, and other service types of activity, and not manufacturing, than in the second city.

C. GROUPS IN THE POLITICAL PROCESS

THE POLITICAL ROLE OF ORGANIZED GROUPS

For the student of politics, the important thing about social groups is the political role they play. Accordingly, it will help to bear in mind several basic distinctions. In the first place, one should distinguish between "groups" that are simply aggregates of people conveniently described by the same set of terms, and "groups" that are

[3] The latter rivalry should be familiar to North Americans, being typical of politics at the state level, although the former, rivalry between the two leading cities, characterizes the politics of Missouri and California.

[4] In Brazil this situation will presumably be modified in the future by the recent move of the federal capital to Brasilia.

actually organized, with a leadership structure and specific common interests that give rise to common political aims. Thus one can discuss Latin American children of school age, or Bolivian Presidents of the nineteenth century, as "categoric groups," as aggregates of people with common characteristics who can be considered together; they are not "purposive groups," with leadership, organization, and specific functions to perform. It is with purposive groups that we are at present concerned.

The type of political activity in which groups engage will clearly depend on the stage of development at which the country's political life has arrived. As the country progresses further from the turmoil that followed its establishment as an independent state, as it develops political institutions capable of resolving disputes by peaceful means —assuming that it ever does—the methods of political activity become those appropriate to a stable and peaceful society. This change in appropriate political techniques means a change in the types of groups that are important in the state's political life. Obviously, if force is the only technique usable in settling disputes, for example, the army will be of crucial importance. The political importance of the army, accordingly, diminishes as a state develops politically.

However, force in politics need not consist only of fighting pitched battles. The general strike, for example, is a use of force that may be effective, and organized labor can wield political power even in an era dominated by violent methods. Other groups, too, may be in a strategic position to make effective use of the strike, as the section on political violence below endeavors to make clear.

In the succeeding stages of political evolution, then, ability to use techniques other than those of violence becomes more important in determining the role a group will play in politics. As voting strength becomes substituted for fighting capabilities in measuring a group's bargaining power, numbers assume a new significance. The importance of sheer numbers, however, will be modified by other factors. This is obviously the case where suffrage is limited, say to the literate, as is currently the case in Brazil, Chile, Colombia, Peru, and Ecuador.

The importance of sheer numbers is also modified by the relative presence or absence of the appropriate skills among the group's leadership. For example: the National Confederation of Popular Organizations, one of the three "sectors" of the government political party in Mexico, does well for itself out of proportion to its membership in intra-party bargaining over party nominations to office, in part because its leaders are especially skilled in the arts appropriate to successful private negotiations. One recalls the aphorism that the United States has never lost a war and never won a peace conference.

A final variable that will help determine a group's relative political importance is the extent to which the group's claims are consistent with the felt imperatives of national interest. That is, if it is the settled policy of the state to pursue a program of economic development requiring the expansion of domestic industry, local businessmen are in a strong position to press their political claims. If an increase in the number of people speaking foreign languages were clearly in the national interest, say, the teachers of foreign languages would find themselves in a strong tactical position.

BUSINESS GROUPS

There are several features of the activity of business interests as political groups in Latin America that deserve special mention. Typically, there exists in each of the republics a general association of business leaders in manufacturing and commerce that will concern itself with public issues that affect business as a whole. General labor legislation, for example, would be one such issue.

For many purposes, however, associations of firms engaged in specific types of activity, and individual businessmen, are more likely to be involved in the formulation and administration of any given governmental policy than the business community as a whole. This takes place because most government action that affects the country's economy will have varying impacts on different types of business. A country's tariff, for example, the formulation of which is one of the key areas of public policy as far as business interests are concerned, typically applies different rates to different items of trade.

Each manufacturing industry lobbies for protection from foreign competition for its own product, and while the interests of different industries may well coincide on tariff questions, they are often in conflict. Similarly, different industries may oppose each other on tax questions, saying in effect "Tax him, not me."

Moreover, business is also interested in government contracts, and here, of course, activity is necessarily on an individual firm basis, with firms competing with each other for government favor. Subsidies and special economic legislation of all kinds likewise come in this general category.

If one were to group businessmen in terms of their political orientation, however, the following broad classification might have some merit. The first business group, which might be called "traditional," is composed of owners and managerial staffs of enterprises not engaged in manufacturing, but in the public utilities field, in railroads and shipping, banking, insurance, mining, and the representation of foreign interests. These are the traditional non-agricultural economic activities in Latin America; they are also those involving connections with foreign, that is, European and North American, business interests. Here representatives of the old upper classes are to be found, and often outlooks on life similar to those prevailing among the large landowners.

A second sector of the business community, the "new" group, let us say, is composed of entrepreneurs in industries that developed to serve the domestic market, especially during World War II, when consumer goods were in scarce supply from the industrialized countries, whose economies were engaged in war production. A comparable development, of lesser magnitude, had occurred during the first World War, and even a little earlier. As always in the first stages of industrialization, industries began first to provide goods that are in need even where the population subsists at a low level: food, clothing, and housing. The first industries, accordingly, are invariably food processing, soft drink and beer manufacturing, cement, and textiles. Some activity during this initial stage in the production of other articles of prime necessity—matches, cigarettes, and soap, for example.

During World War II, and in the years since then, however, the process went further than this, especially in Mexico and Brazil, the countries with the largest domestic markets, where today a wide variety of goods are produced, for domestic consumption and export to neighboring states. Argentina and Uruguay have also experienced considerable industrial development, dating from earlier in the century.

Businessmen of the "new" group come to a lesser extent from the old upper classes, one major reason for this being that the new industries are often located near sources of raw materials or power, or central distribution points, away from the capital.

Where he depends principally on the domestic market for his sales, the businessman of this type favors tariff protection against foreign competition, and is more likely to support moves of "economic nationalism" in general.

The third group within the business community might be designated "petty" business, comprising the self-employed in trade and services who are not themselves significant employers of labor. The taxi drivers, owners of tiny grocery stores, shoemakers, and so on, of this group, make up a surprisingly large proportion of the economically active urban population. At its margins, this group blends into the ordinary labor force, and the political aims and methods of its members are closer to those of organized labor than to those of other business groups. That is, members of the group lack direct personal access to individuals in high authority on the one hand, but on the other hand are numerous enough to have an impact at the polls, and by means of rallies and strikes. At the same time, the low income level of the petty businessman makes him highly concerned, like the laborer, with the general level of prices and of government benefits.

Quite commonly, one must point out, relations between individual firms and public officials in Latin America are based on bribery and betrayal of the public trust. In the dictatorships, the existence of this situation is well known, of course. Of the recent dictators, Perón in Argentina, Batista in Cuba, Trujillo in the Dominican Republic, and Pérez Jiménez in Venezuela, amassed fortunes reckoned in the hundreds of millions of dollars; Anastasio Somoza, in Nicaragua, became a millionaire probably on a lesser scale.

Graft through illicit government-business connections is not unknown in the democratic countries either; Brazil and Mexico, and Panama among the smaller countries, have a particularly impressive reputation on this score, although this is hardly a point on which comparative annual statistics can be published.

A great deal more "business graft" becomes available when a country embarks on a program of economic development. Fortunes can be made quite simply as an incident of a government program of encouraging the development of industry. Attempts have been made to justify "North American" graft of this type, which at least is associated with the productive use of government funds, as opposed to classic "Latin" graft which simply entails the plundering of tax revenues, with no economic development involved.

As an illustration of how "constructive" graft works, the recent notable case of a leading Mexican figure may be cited. This political leader, who once missed nomination for the Presidency by the merest accident, was given, together with a group of associates, a sizeable government loan to start a paper-making concern. The group was also given exclusive rights to cut timber in a national forest. Moreover, a prohibitive tariff was placed on certain foreign paper products, despite the fact that they were in short supply in Mexico. Government help on this extensive a scale is almost as good as a license to print money. From one point of view, this is corruption; from another, it is economic development and the industrialization process. After all, initial industrial development in Japan, and in the United States too, was heavily government-subsidized (and often still is). Thus the administration of President Alemán in Mexico (1946-52), himself now a very rich man, was on the one hand a period of colossal industrial growth and public building in the country, and, on the other, the era in which graft reached new orders of magnitude.

In general, then, business's political activity is more likely to be conducted by individuals, single firms, and single industries than on a unified basis. In terms of the techniques business groups can employ, clearly *by itself* the business community commands neither military or para-military force, nor numbers of votes. Accordingly, the techniques business usually uses are those involving personal influence, campaign contributions, bribery, and the giving or withholding of cooperation on government programs that require such cooperation—those involving holding down prices, obeying labor laws, paying taxes promptly, for example.

ORGANIZED LABOR

The age of the national labor movement varies, in general, with the country's over-all level of political advance. Labor unions as we know them today go back to the nineteenth century in Chile and Uruguay. The union movement in Honduras, on the other hand, is scarcely 10 years old, and Haiti's less than 20. The types of economic activity in which workers are engaged determines how feasible it is to organize them (this can be seen also in the United States, for example, with respect to migrant farm workers), with agricultural workers being especially difficult to organize—because they are not so concentrated into one spot; because the rural areas are out of the mainstream of national life; because agriculture is less productive than industry and presents fewer possibilities of workers' gaining through organization; and because of the political power of the landowner class, which has often secured legislation making union organization more difficult among rural workers, or outlawing it entirely. In about a third of the republics, there are still no organizations of agricultural workers.

A substantial increase in the number of workers enlisted in union ranks has been noticeable since World War II, following in part on the acceleration in the rate of industrialization during the war period.

Transportation and public services exist, of course, even in the pre-industrial era, although there may be legal prohibition of the unionization of government employees and such services are often government-provided. Nevertheless, railroad workers were generally one of the first groups to be organized in the Latin American countries, sometimes preceded by the printers' trades. Restrictions on the organization of government employees are widespread, and even where unionization is allowed, the right of public workers to strike is typically limited. There are obvious reasons why this should be so.

Organized labor has always been "in politics" in Latin America since the early years, following the European pattern rather than adopting the traditional North American "business unionism" principle of confining activities to securing economic benefits with a minimum of involvement in party politics. European influences were in fact strong in the Latin American labor movement in its early years. Societies of handworkers existed as early as the middle of the nineteenth century with mutual aid and insurance purposes, providing protection against sickness and burial expenses, and serving as fraternal and self-help organizations. Workers' groups became politically-minded under the influence of Spanish and Italian immigrants late in the century, taking on the utopian, anarchist, and syndicalist coloration of the early unions in France, Spain, and Italy; that is, the dominant political doctrines did not envisage political action within the society and polity as then constituted, but only an apocalyptic act, sometime in the future—the general strike—to bring about the collapse of capitalist society and its replacement by some other type of society, conceived of in rather vague terms, which would operate without compulsion and human exploitation.

Around the turn of the century, specifically socialist ideas began to become progressively stronger in the labor movement, being joined by a separate Communist tendency after the Bolshevik Revolution. The more militant Communist element, while always in the minority, did become very potent during the 1930s, when Communists occupied key positions in unions in many of the Latin American countries, as they did elsewhere too at the time. This strength has since receded, although not disappeared, as a result of several factors: attrition in Communist ranks themselves as the basic requirement of loyalty to the Soviet Union took Communist parties along a twisting and often unpopular line of policy; government policies on the one hand restricting the Party's activities or outlawing it altogether, and on the other hand pursuing a liberal line that undercut Communism's appeal; and a vigorous counterattack by democratic socialist and left-liberal forces within the unions themselves, with some aid from the North American union movement and the regional free trade union federation (ORIT). Separate Christian unions have also been formed in recent years, acquiring political significance in Chile, and promising to become of increasing importance elsewhere, for example, in Argentina and Central America.

There are currently interesting but isolated cases of new labor federations established with at least the intention of sticking to bread-and-butter economic activities and staying out of politics, in Colombia and very recently in Mexico. One may perhaps be pardoned for viewing the prospects for a non-political labor movement in Latin America with a jaundiced eye, however, since the growth of the labor movement has in the past been very clearly related to government favor or disfavor. Thus, the most highly unionized republics—those with the highest proportion of manual workers actually belonging to unions—have been Cuba and Argentina. This state of affairs is clearly due to the official support of the union movement in the 1930s and 1940s in Cuba under Batista, Grau San Martín, and Prío Socarras, and in the 1940s and 1950s in Argentina under Perón.

The attitude of the government is crucial not only because it establishes the ground rules that apply to the organization of unions (compare the differences between the effects of the Wagner, Taft-Hartley, and Landrum-Griffin Acts in the United States), but because it takes a hand in day-to-day union activity and collective bargaining. Typically, official approval is necessary for a strike; if the strike is declared illegal, strikers may be fired without reinstatement rights, and if the strike threatens to damage the national economy seriously, the government may even suppress it by violent means. On the other hand, the government board charged with labor conciliation may find that the demands of the workers are justified, and the President or the legislature may embody them in decrees or legislation. The settling of a labor dispute by Presidential decree is a common occurrence.

Obviously, under these circumstances, it pays heavy dividends to be on good terms with the incumbent administration, which, for its part, will require in return loyalty from the union federation. Sometimes the government will take direct action to ensure such loyalty, or at least to interdict anti-government policies, on the part of the unions. Argentine unions, for example, were "intervened" freely by Perón, in the days when he was establishing his control over the labor movement, and later by President Aramburu in trying to purge the union leadership of Peronist elements. "Intervention" consists of suspending the union's officials from their functions, which are taken over by a government-appointed interventor.

The history of Mexican political life provides ample illustration of official control of the union movement's being established by means of the favoring of one federation and one set of leaders over another. During President Calles' term (1924-28), for example, the CROM, under Luis Morones, who became a sort of Mexican Jimmy Hoffa, was given government protection and favor and waxed great and arrogant. Morones was frozen out of his privileged position, however, by Emilio Portes Gil, Provisional President during 1929, and subsequently under President Cárdenas official favor was accorded Vicente Lombardo Toledano, an intellectual who headed the rival CTM. Lombardo was too radical for Cárdenas's successors in office, though (the federation he now heads is affiliated with the Communist international labor movement), and he was forced out of the position of favored labor leader, yielding it to the present general secretary of the CTM, Fidel Velásquez.

Labor organization in Latin America is covered, like many other areas of activity, with an extensive system of public regulation, often of the most minute details of union affairs. Like other such detailed codes of regulation, however, it is typically only partially enforced, and then politically, that is, government supporters are favored, opponents not. Working conditions, maximum hours of work, minimum rates of pay, retirement, sickness and disability benefits, and grievance procedures are covered by the labor codes; these codes are enforced often against large-scale foreign enterprises, rarely against domestic business, and hardly ever against rural landowners. The foreign enterprise, that is, is easy to regulate; highly visible, affluent enough to meet the terms specified by law, without popular domestic support, and with a rational accounting system that simplifies enforcement of the regulations.

As was noted above, governments in power favor labor not only out of principle, but also in the expectation of benefiting from future labor support. Thus, the relationship between the two may entail not only the protection and direct encouragement of unionization, but also the subsequent organization of unionized workers in a pro-government political party. The early Revolutionary governments of Mexico had fostered the growth of a labor movement, and subsequently the major labor federation affiliated directly with the government party, now the Party of Revolutionary Institutions, when President Calles founded it in 1928. Juan D. Perón, similarly, made the fostering of new unions one of the primary policies of the early days of his regime, and then used the unions as the basis for the *Peronista* Party. Likewise, Getúlio Vargas, the Brazilian dictator, founded the *Partido Trabalhista Brasileiro,* after he had left the Presidency, out of elements supporting him because of his pro-labor policies. During Fulgencio Batista's earlier period of dominance of Cuban politics (to 1944), he too built a political party, with the participation of unions whose growth he had promoted. All of the Presidents cited were soldiers who came to power originally in a military context and secured the adherence of labor elements by virtue of the policies they pursued after they took office.

Labor unions are in a strategic political position for various reasons, and increasingly governments in search of popular support have turned to organized labor. In the first place, labor can generally command a substantial bloc of votes in the balloting. In any case, the organized character of the labor movement, and the number of people whose mobilization for election-time and other political tasks it makes possible, is itself significant in view of the general lack of continuing party organization in Latin America. More important still is the power of the strike weapon, which can be used for purposes ranging from the backing up of a demand for a wage increase to the overthrow of a government. Accordingly, the position of the labor movement has become one of the central features in the politics of almost all of the Latin American countries. In the case of Bolivia, for example, one could truthfully say that the tin miners constitute the most important single political force in the country.

AGRICULTURE

In all the countries of the area except Haiti, Costa Rica, and Mexico, with Bolivia and Cuba now transitional cases, the chief agricultural interest is that of the large landowner, the owner of the huge *fazenda, finca, estancia,* or *hacienda,* as it is variously known. The landowner is a potent figure in national politics. The labor laws are not written to cover the people who work for him, or if they are, they are not enforced. The tax burden rests but lightly on his shoulders.

In his country's politics the aim of the large landowner, as a class, is to be left alone—that is, for the rural *status quo* not to be disturbed. In his view, the role of government with respect to agriculture should be supportive, not restrictive—to provide subsidies, tariffs, and loans whose repayment is not stringently insisted upon.

In the coastal lowlands of the tropical areas around the Caribbean, one finds plantation crops—sugar, bananas, cacao, cotton—very often grown by North American concerns. Historically, these concerns, too, had a powerful voice in politics and operated outside the law. The government-manipulating exploits of the banana-growing buccaneer, Samuel Zemurray, in Central America, have long been regarded as typical of the operations of United States fruit companies. Today, although United Fruit and its subsidiaries and affiliates still loom large in the economies and politics of the Caribbean, governments that want to have learned how to domesticate the fruit companies. In banana-growing Ecuador and Panama, at least, the government keeps United Fruit in its place, enforcing the labor laws, for example, against it even if against no one else. However, laws in Guatemala and Honduras are less restrictive toward United Fruit, and governments there are more likely to consult with the company than to fight it. North American interests in agriculture have been expropriated in Cuba, on the other hand, and largely so in Mexico. In Panama, United Fruit's subsidiary has even threatened to stop operations in the country if it is saddled with further financial obligations to the government or to its own workers. One cannot assume that this threat is an idle one, moreover. United Fruit has found it better economics to limit the bulk of its operations in Ecuador to shipping and marketing the stems, rather than growing them, and has shown signs of adopting this policy elsewhere.

Where the *hacienda* system is in full effect, agricultural laborers—the forgotten men of the nation—have no voice in politics. If thoroughgoing land reform should come, however, as it doubtless will to many countries in the area, the ex-tenants, -sharecroppers, or -laborers receiving land under the program will gain a political voice along with the title to their parcel.[5] In Mexico the organized beneficiaries of the land reform constitute one of the sectors of the government political party, and any government must make a special effort to be *agrarista* in its policies. In Bolivia, the *campesinos* (the peasants), most of whom have seized land without waiting for the formalities involved in receiving a title, are much more loosely organized but still constitute one of the key elements in national politics. These new landowners are interested in credit, irrigation

[5] The economics and politics of land reform programs will be dealt with at greater length in a subsequent chapter, in relation to its role in an economic development policy.

projects, rural schools and perhaps extension programs, and price supports. They also champion the right to receive land of those peasants who have not yet benefited from the land reform.

In Haiti ownership of the land has always been widely distributed, since shortly after Independence, and the problem of reform of the land tenure system has not arisen. The small landowner is also typical of much of Costa Rica, Panama, and some areas of Colombia, although the precise figures are in dispute.

In Uruguay, until very recently, an unusual situation existed. Agriculture—in this case principally livestock production—instead of being subsidized, directly and indirectly, as in most of the other states in the area, was itself forced to subsidize Uruguayan industry. Uruguay, under the Colorado party, had long followed the policy of favoring industrial development, but since the country's manufacturing proved a high-cost enterprise, domestic raw materials and power not being available, it could only develop with heavy government aid of various types. The ultimate source of this financing of industry was government profits from the state's monopoly on agricultural and pastoral exports. Uruguayan farmers would of course sooner have received all the benefits from the export of their products themselves, and rural dissatisfaction with Colorado economic policies was one of the key factors in the defeat of the party in 1958, after half a century in power. The Blanco regime has yet to demonstrate that it can manage Uruguay's economy better—or even as well —as the Colorados, however.

The structure of a country's land tenure system depends in part on the crops grown—tobacco and coffee, for example, can normally be grown just as profitably on a small farm as on a large one, whereas sugar or cotton are more rationally cultivated on a plantation basis—and this will in turn depend on the terrain, the soil, and the climate. For instance, the best coffee is grown in temperate highland areas with porous volcanic soil, as in El Salvador or Colombia, whereas the rolling grasslands of Uruguay are ideal for cattle-grazing. Thus, specific local factors go to shape a country's system of land tenure. One would nevertheless be justified in asserting that at present, just as 100 years ago, with the exceptions noted on the preceding pages, the typical Latin American landholding unit is the *latifundia,* the extremely large estate only partially farmed by a miserable resident laboring force, using primitive, low-yield, tradition-bound methods.

This basic situation maintains and reinforces the social structure and attitudes discussed earlier, and creates problems for economic policy that will be considered in the final chapter. In political terms, it means the presence of an extremely influential group opposed to virtually any kind of social and political change, whose power is absolute on the local level in the rural districts of four-fifths of the republics, and on the national level in several of them.

STUDENTS

Student groups are of key importance in Latin American politics. Student politics are integrated with national politics; student body elections are fought among candidates identified with the national political parties; leadership of a major student faction in the national university carries national political prominence; the holding of elected office in the student government is the first step in a political career. At the same time, university issues become of national moment, and the chain of events that leads to the overthrow of a government may have had its origin in the appointment of an unpopular rector (the chief university administrator); while the President of the Republic may find himself called on to decide how many applicants the Medical School should admit, or what the student fare on buses should be.

The Latin American university, with one or two rare exceptions, has little in common with the university in the United States, so far as its organization and the status of its student body are concerned. In North American universities, the administration, which is separate from both faculty and student body and is normally responsible to an outside body of some kind, frequently prescribes detailed regulations governing the life of the student, often of a highly paternalistic kind. Autonomous student life and student government have to do only with trivial matters and private social activities.

The Latin American university is actually much more similar, in many ways, to that of medieval Europe—that is, an association of scholars regulating their own affairs. In fact, the oldest major institutions of learning in the hemisphere—the Universities of San Marcos in Lima, of Santo Domingo, and of Mexico City—date from the middle of the sixteenth century. However, contemporary student participation in university government dates properly from the University Reform movement, which began in Argentina during the second decade of the twentieth century, and had as concomitant aims the relaxation of academic regulations, the introduction of extension programs, and the general democratization of the university. Today, the Latin American university is not completely controlled by the students, certainly, but they do have a share in its actual policy-making and administration, and not only in trivial affairs. For example, student participation occurs in the election of the rectors of the several faculties (the colleges devoted to specific branches of learning). Student representatives commonly account for between one-fifth and one-third of the membership of important university councils and committees.

Usually the government has a role in university administration, often designating the rector or at least representatives on university boards. This means that the government is involved in university politics, just as students are in national politics.

In effect, the student community in a national university, especially in the faculties of law, philosophy, and the social sciences (where a separate faculty for the latter exists), is the group that constitutes, with its alumni, the nation's political elite. The prominence of a substantial number of the present political leaders of the Latin American republics began at the university. Rómulo Betancourt, at the time of writing President of Venezuela, as well as the leader of the major opposition party to Betancourt, Jóvito Villalba, both started in politics as student leaders in the 1930s. Fidel Castro Ruz first came into public view as the candidate for the Vice-Presidency of the student body in the Faculty of Law at the University of Havana, and his associates in his first act of rebellion against the Batista dictatorship, the assault on the Moncada Barracks, were former fellow-students.

Some political movements have been organized among the students by their professors, sometimes initially as aids in a campaign for the office of rector. The present President of Bolivia, Víctor Paz Estenssoro, organized his *Movimiento Nacional Revolucionario* as a Professor of Economics in La Paz. Former President Grau San Martín of Cuba also organized his initial political following among his students at the university.

Because of the importance of student politics, one often finds superannuated nominal students prolonging their university course far past its normal term so that they can continue active in university politics, even deliberately failing their examinations if necessary to maintain student status. Some individuals continue as students more or less indefinitely, perhaps switching to a new field and starting over after receiving a degree, waiting for the government to change to the control of their own party and for a political career to open up.

Actually, appointment to a government job may well seem the only prospect for many students. Concentrating in the humanities, especially literature and philosophy, and in law, students are not particularly being trained for the specialties in demand, while in any case there is typically general unemployment and underemployment in all sectors of the economy. An appointment to the diplomatic service or to a post in the Ministry of Education may represent the only hope for lucrative employment to the undergraduate poet or philosopher; the lawyers are more versatile, but there are too many of them, also.

This involvement with national politics means frequent hiatuses in the normal pursuit of one's studies. The student body may be out on strike in protest against a government, or a university, policy; the school may be closed by the government, as a precautionary measure or in retaliation for a student strike or demonstration. Professors or students may be absent from the classroom under arrest, or leading a revolt, or presenting demands to the President. Students from the United States have been known to give up in bafflement after trying unsuccessfully to pursue a course of study for a term at a Latin American institution.

In recent years, there has been something of a trend to a more North American type of university, in some respects, in the "university city" movement. In Mexico, Cuba, and Panama, universities have been relocated on campuses of their own away from their traditional home downtown in the national capital.[6]

The politics of the university student are in general more extreme than the politics of the adult world. Specifically, the student's political orientation is more likely to be nationalist, Leftist, and Marxist. This is so for various reasons. The idealism of youth, which one must surely commend without necessarily agreeing with the specific views to which it gives rise, means a position on the Left except where strong religious feelings supervene; at the same time the intellectual apparatus of Marxism appeals strongly to the intellectual, and its anti-U. S. implications make it still more attractive; while the rebelliousness that naturally accompanies later youth is augmented by the gulf between the generations typical of the Hispanic family.

At the same time, the class position and prospects of the student have a great deal to do with his political outlook. The children of well-to-do families frequently go abroad for their education, to Europe or the United States. Fees in the national universities are

[6] The present writer is more than a little inclined to suspect that in constructing "university cities" governments are not simply endeavoring to create the most favorable environment for learning, but are also trying to save themselves a lot of headaches by de-politicizing the university, at least by getting it away from the vicinity of the Presidential and Legislative Palaces and thereby insuring that a student demonstration will not automatically place the life of the government in jeopardy. It may be relevant in this connection to note that the trend to the "university city" has also entailed an emphasis on athletics which is totally new for Latin American universities, and may provide an interest- and energy-absorbing alternative to participation in political demonstrations.

usually nominal; students there are often poor, not only supporting themselves but also in many cases contributing something to their families—university attendance is normally a part-time proposition. In other words, the student is often undergoing genuine hardship, working too hard or too long at his outside job, and, as noted above, his prospects for remunerative employment in his field at graduation are slim. The resentment and frustration that grow from this situation contribute their share to a politics of emotional extremism.

Thus, one might almost generalize that the students are always against the government, regardless of its complexion and policies.

The more conservative faculties, as one would expect, are Engineering and Medicine. There the students are not so intellectual nor so socially conscious as those in the other faculties and can look forward to relatively easier access to prosperous careers.

The religious influence is stronger in provincial universities, which are as a rule less politicized than those in the national capitals; but conditions vary so widely that it is hard to generalize on this point.

THE URBAN POOR

In the last 20 years, the cities of Latin America have experienced phenomenal growth. The doubling of urban populations during this period has not been exceptional. The rate of growth of the cities has been so rapid that the supply of decent housing has been completely swamped, and in many cases the provision of municipal facilities has been strained past the breaking point. Guayaquil, in Ecuador, has perhaps suffered most from the ills of urban population explosion, but Rio and Caracas also show extreme symptoms, and no major city is immune.

The new arrivals from the countryside improvise shacks out of whatever materials are available, and settlements of such dwellings mushroom around the outskirts of the city, unprovided with water, electricity, or sewage disposal facilities. Little employment is available—the city population was rapidly expanding anyhow by the natural increase of its inhabitants—and the dweller in the *rancho* or the *favela* lives in conditions of misery, hopelessness, and general social disorganization. There were already miserable unemployed and underemployed in the city, but now the order of magnitude of the problem is changed.

The political activity of the slumdweller is at present minimal—he is apathetic and "alienated" from the political process—and today he is most logically considered as a social problem rather than a social force, as object, not as subject. This situation is unlikely to last indefinitely, however.

D. THE ARMY AND POLITICAL VIOLENCE

THE VARYING ROLES OF THE ARMY

As everyone knows, the armies of Latin America are involved in the politics of their countries. The precise nature of the involvement shows a good deal of significant variation, however, in kind as well as in degree, and the whole topic has been subject to much misunderstanding. We must then discuss the political role of the army in Latin America in terms of the different types of "involvement in politics" that are possible for military organizations.

Minimal Involvement in Politics. Now, virtually any army is involved in politics at least as a pressure group acting in the interests of its constituents. That is, it is interested in the procurement of the most modern weapons, in securing increases in pay and fringe benefits, in building officers' clubs, and so on. We are not unfamiliar with this type of military lobbying in the United States, of course, nor with *sub rosa* contacts between military officers and legislators, nor even with generals' making speeches on policy questions, despite the well-established doctrine of civilian control, and despite repeated attempts of the civilian leadership to keep the military confined to their professional functions.

In Uruguay this pressure group role is normally the extent of military involvement in politics, and in Chile and Mexico military involvement does not go much further than this. Actually, in Costa Rica, which has no army as such, and only a small national police, one can hardly speak even of this minimal a military involvement;

and perhaps not in Bolivia, where the Revolution of 1952 virtually destroyed the army and the surviving remnant has been kept out of political activity. The maintenance of internal order in Bolivia is the function of a militia of the government party, the M. N. R., which, at least to the time of writing, has developed no political personality independent of the party. Developments in Cuba have been similar in form to those of Bolivia, with the destruction of the army that existed prior to the assumption of power by Fidel Castro at the beginning of 1959, and the substitution for it of a revolutionary army and militia, so far at one with the revolutionary movement and its leadership. It remains to be seen how long the "party armies" of Cuba and Bolivia will remain without a separate corporate identity of their own that will make it possible for divergences of outlook to appear between them and the revolutionary governments. The example of developments in the revolutionary armies of other countries, from Mexico to the Soviet Union, suggest that, sooner or later, that time will come.

The Military as Guardians of the Constitution. A stage much further into political activity than simple "pressure group" behavior has been reached when the army identifies itself as guardian of the nation's constitution. Acting in this role, the military are not interested in imposing some change in direction on government policy and certainly not in ruling; they merely act to protect constitutional procedures and civil rights—*even, paradoxically, where this means intervening against the legally constituted civilian leadership.* The outsider should think twice before condemning this type of activity, which can be quite public-spirited and disinterested, and generally welcomed by the citizenry. Is it the more honorable or commendable path to stand by while a President, even one legally elected, converts his regime into a tyranny when you have the ability to turn him out of office? Many officers have searched their consciences, answered "no," and subsequently been blessed for it by their countrymen. The recent dictatorships of Perón, Rojas Pinilla, and Pérez Jiménez, for example, were brought to an end by the action of soldiers who did not believe that the doctrine of the subordination of the military to the republic's elected leadership should be interpreted to the advantage of tyrants.

In the view of the present writer, at least, one should thus not condemn all military interventions out of hand but should first look to see against whom they were directed. To remove a Pérez Jiménez from office can surely only be a patriotic act, by any standard.

It remains true, however, that the presumption should always be against the military *coup d'état*. It represents a violation of legality, sets a bad precedent, and induces or strengthens an unhealthy and unprofessional attitude among the soldiers. Even a *coup* staged with the purpose of restoring the country to democracy needs to be eyed askance; the military can be quite naive about politics, and may have misjudged the character of the incumbent regime by misunderstanding the alternatives available to it. Then, too, the new military leadership may itself succumb to the temptations of power, as in the case of Rojas Pinilla—and of course the announced high purposes of the *coup* may be simply a disguise to mask the transition to a worse dictatorship than the one overthrown. Nevertheless, examples of the beneficent military *coup* do exist.

After the military overthrow of a tyrant, the true "guardian of the constitution" rules only provisionally until the heritage of the dictatorship can be liquidated, political life revived, orderly elections held, and the country returned to civilian authority. That has indeed occurred at the political demise of Rojas Pinilla, Pérez Jiménez, and Perón, and it would be difficult to contend that General Aramburu or Admiral Rojas, say, who were in the leadership of the revolt against Perón, had acted other than honorably.

It has occurred, of course, that after a dictator has been overthrown in a military *coup,* popular adulation has gone to the head of the general who delivered the crucial ultimatum, and he has decided to hold on to power himself, rather than return it to civilian hands at the earliest opportunity. This seems the most plausible explanation for the actions of Rojas Pinilla of Colombia, who originally earned the people's gratitude by his overthrow of the tyrannical Laureano Gómez, only to earn their later opprobrium by his own conduct in office. In this case Rojas Pinilla overstepped the bounds of the role of "guardian of the institution," became himself a dictator continuing in office by force and fraud, and must be judged accordingly.

The military in Brazil have traditionally assumed the role—often consciously and explicitly—of "guardians of the constitution." Perhaps the army has felt responsible for the republican constitution, since it was the army that forced Dom Pedro II to abdicate in 1889, brought the republic into existence, and provided its first President in Deodoro da Fonseca. It was the armed forces, again, that escorted Getúlio Vargas from his dictatorial Presidency in 1945. In recent years, the Brazilian army's distinctive conception of its constitutional role has resulted in some curious involvements on its part in the skirmishing around the President's chair.

In 1955, for example, Marshal Lott's famous "preventive" *coup d'état* occurred. The candidates on the winning ticket in the Presidential elections of that year, Juscelino Kubitschek and João Goulart, were strongly opposed by some Army leaders as too Leftist, and a *coup* that would forestall their inauguration was in the making. José Café Filho, who had become President on the suicide of the incumbent, again Getúlio Vargas, resigned; the then Acting President, Carlos Luz, dismissed Marshal Henrique Teixeira Lott from his post as Minister of War to smooth the path of the projected *coup*. Lott, for his part, staged a counter-*coup,* dismissed Luz, and, figuratively speaking, presided over the ceremonies that inaugurated Kubitschek and Goulart. Lott's action thus constitutes the classic example of the paradox of a *coup d'état* that protects the constitution.

A parallel situation in many respects was created at the resignation of the President who succeeded Kubitschek, Jânio Quadros, in August of 1961. The chiefs of the armed services tried to bring pressure to prevent the accession to the Presidency of Goulart, who had been re-elected Vice-President. Lott, now a private citizen (he had run for the Presidency unsuccessfully against Quadros), taking a position similar to the one he had adopted six years before, was jailed for denouncing the maneuver, which eventually failed in the face of popular opposition, the refusal of some key subordinate military commanders to follow the lead of the service chiefs, and the mobilization for civil war of Goulart's home state of Rio Grande do Sul. On this occasion it was their subordinates, and not the military chiefs, who successfully defended constitutional norms by disobeying orders.

In recent years the Ecuadorean army, too, has seen itself in the role of "defender of the constitution." On no fewer than three occasions (in 1935, 1947, and 1961), the army has forced the resignation of perennial President José María Velasco Ibarra for unpopular and dictatorial measures he had taken; yet it has not itself assumed control of the government on these occasions, except in 1947 and then only on a provisional basis to organize elections. On the other hand, when Velasco exercised restraint and functioned more or less within the constitution, he was allowed to serve out his term peacefully (1952-56). Other Presidents who stayed within constitutional limits —Galo Plaza Lasso (1948-52) and Camilo Ponce Enríquez (1956-60) —have also completed their terms without army intervention. Velasco had in fact been inaugurated for his second term under army auspices, after the armed forces had ejected the dictator Arroyo del Río (1940-44).

The Military as Holders of a Veto Power. More often than not, however, the generals and admirals who get involved in politics do not confine their activities to preventing violations of the constitution only (or at all), but use pressure to get their way on questions of policy. This brings us to the third type of role the military can play: as wielder of a veto power. In a situation of this character, civilians rule, in all likelihood those elected by constitutional procedures; quite possibly civil liberties are preserved; perhaps most of government policy is determined by the elected leadership. Nevertheless, the government remains in power only on the sufferance of the military, and cannot afford to antagonize the armed forces. Major decisions are first discussed with the leading military commanders, and their advice taken. In effect, they wield a veto on policy. Decisions of the civilian leadership. in other words, are made only within the limits tolerated by the army.

Perhaps a half a dozen states headed, since the fall of Perón in 1955, by Argentina, come more or less into this category. The President makes policy but is figuratively always looking over his shoulder to observe the reactions of the military leaders. This is especially the case where the government lives under continual threat of overthrow, and must rely on the army to put down popular manifestations. This was the situation in which Arturo Frondizi of Argentina found himself during his brief and eventful term, which was brought to an untimely close by military intervention at the beginning of April, 1962. Frondizi not only had to work within the limits acceptable to his military chiefs, but he was compelled to change policies already embarked upon under open military pressure. Such a change, quite clear to public view, was forced in the position he had taken on the suspension of Cuba from the Organization of American States shortly before his eventual downfall.

Rómulo Betancourt of Venezuela has been in a rather similar position; existing under continual attack from both Left and Right, and without a popular majority in the city of Caracas, the country's capital, the Betancourt government could hardly survive without continuing unequivocal military support. In recent years, Panama, Peru, Honduras, and Guatemala have also been in the category of states in which the military is one of the country's key political forces, a civilian government must always take the wishes of the military into account, and from time to time the military intervenes to eject a government over a policy or personnel dispute.

Military Rule. A category of civil-military relationships not uncommonly met with in Latin America is that of simple military rule: army officers openly occupy the leading positions. The pure case under this heading is Paraguay, where the President is never a civilian and the regime never other than a dictatorship. The Rojas Pinilla regime in Colombia, which openly referred to itself as "the government of the armed forces," fell into this category, as did that of Manuel Odría in Peru.

Pure military rule is most commonly found in the small tropical countries of the area—Paraguay, and the Central American and Caribbean republics—and is attributable in a general way to the lack of political maturity and the generally rudimentary stage of social and political development reached in those republics. The distinctive characteristics of the "pure" military dictatorship are normally that the President is one of the army's ranking generals and holds the Presidential office by virtue of his military standing; that the support of no civilian political group is committed to him personally; and that he shares the power of political decision with other senior officers.

From this position of chief military representative, of trustee of power for the army, the military dictator may build up his *personal* power, outmaneuver his military colleagues, and emerge as a personal dictator. This was especially easy for Rafael Trujillo in the Dominican Republic and Anastasio Somoza in Nicaragua, each being the first commanding general of his country's newly reorganized and re-trained armed forces when the occupation of his country by the U. S. Marines was liquidated. The personal nature of the rule that each enjoyed for over a generation was clearly illustrated by the striking parallels in the way the career of each was ended; each was removed only by assassination, Somoza in 1956, Trujillo in 1961, and in both cases the reins of power devolved (in the Trujillo case, only briefly) upon the dictator's son and namesake, who held the rank of Commander-in-Chief. This situation is not an uncommon one: the dictator originally comes to power as corporate representative of the armed forces, but uses his position to establish a personal dictatorship.

The Personal Military Dictator. The final distinct type of military involvement in politics, then, is that involving a personal dictator who springs from the military, but who may not have come to office by virtue of his rank, nor does he rely on the army as his exclusive base of power. In fact, he erects a dictatorship *over* the army, alienating substantial groups within it, which may at the end cause his downfall.

The classic exemplar of this type in recent years is Juan D. Perón, the dictator of Argentina from 1945 to 1955. Marcos Pérez Jiménez of Venezuela (1953-59) and Batista of Cuba are also recent figures in this category. Perón and Pérez Jiménez were both colonels when they started their respective rises to power; the strength of each lay not in his position in the rank list, but in his leadership of a secret lodge of "revolutionary" officers. For his part, Batista vaulted to power originally from the lowly rank of sergeant with the aid of a sort of secret fraternity of N.C.O.'s. Neither Perón nor Pérez Jiménez assumed power immediately after the revolts in which they had played a major role, but each spent some time in a nominally subordinate role, consolidating his power before emerging openly as the regime's Presidential candidate. Similarly, Batista waited seven years (1933-40) before running for President, during which time he exercised his power from behind the scenes.

Perón was highly successful in building support outside the army, particularly among the labor unions, many of which he organized, and whose interests he was assiduous in promoting. He had never enjoyed the united support of the officer corps, and his cultivation of working-class support alienated segments of the military hierarchy even more. Perón also made deliberate attempts to attract the support of other distinct interests in the population—for example, in his initial bid for the allegiance of the devout through the introduction of religious instruction in the schools.

Batista, during his first period in power (he went out of office in 1944, returning by virtue of a *coup d'état* in 1952), and especially during his period in the Presidency, likewise managed to amass popular support, also primarily in the ranks of unionized labor. Although Pérez Jiménez attempted to win favor among civilian groups during the early stages of his regime, his efforts always proved abortive, especially after the monstrous corruption that the possession of power worked in him had begun to appear.

We will have further occasion to discuss the political techniques of Perón, and comparable figures, in the sections on parties and the Presidency.

The definitive establishment of a stable democratic regime necessarily means the strict subordination of military to civilian authority,
and the elimination of military initiatives from politics. This is of
course a task of colossal difficulty. It has been faced not only by
democratic governments in search of stability, but also by dictatorships trying to free themselves from exclusive dependence on military support.

One drastic method of eliminating the army as a political force
is simply to defeat it in combat and disband it forcibly. This is in
effect what has happened, although in quite different contexts, as
the outcome of recent civil wars in Costa Rica in 1948, in Bolivia
in 1952, and in Cuba in 1957-58. In 1948 José Figueres raised the
standard of revolt against the government's attempt to impose its
own choice as President in contravention of the results of the elections. In the ensuing fighting Figueres's movement was successful
and in consequence the Costa Rican army, never very large or significant, was abolished entirely, the only armed force remaining
being the national police, whose numbers and armament are held
to a minimum level consistent with the routine preservation of
domestic peace. In Bolivia the National Revolutionary Movement,
after its victory in the fighting of 1952, disbanded the bulk of the
army, reorganizing the remainder into a small nonpolitical force,
with the responsibility for internal policing resting with an MNR
militia. Fidel Castro's guerrilla forces now constitute the new Cuban
army and militia, ten times as strong, if current reports are to be
believed, as the Batista army which could not overcome them and
no longer exists.

Secondly, the regular military may be checked, in its bent to interfere in politics, by the creation and arming of a counterbalancing
armed force, such as a militia or National Guard. This is actually
the current situation in Honduras, which has, in addition to its regular army, an armed Civil Guard, although its creation has been too
recent for the success of the experiment yet to be evaluated. The

ill-fated government of Jacobo Arbenz Guzmán in Guatemala (1950-53) owed its demise in part to the fact that it was trying to create and arm a militia to forestall its overthrow at some future date by the leadership of the regular army, which was growing restive as a result of the government's far-reaching reform measures. The army refused to train and arm the militia, and Arbenz began to import arms from Eastern Europe, to the chagrin of the United States government; when the country was invaded by a small exile force under Castillo Armas (reputedly with the covert support of the United States' Central Intelligence Agency), the army refused to defend the regime and Arbenz was forced to relinquish his post.

The loyalty of a workers' militia, the "labor battalions" of Mexico City, on the other hand, was partly responsible for the survival of the Obregón government in Mexico in the face of the de la Huerta revolt of 1923. Probably the greater part of the army had gone over to the rebels, but the forces remaining loyal were buttressed by armed workers and the support of peasants who had received land, or anticipated doing so, under the government's agrarian reform program. This was the last revolt in Mexico that had a reasonable chance of succeeding, and marks the watershed, in Mexican history, between an era of turmoil and one of increasing stability. It was only due to the support of what was actually a kind of rudimentary workers' militia, too, that Perón managed to outlast army challenges to his rule, although eventually the armed forces were successful in removing him from office.

In principle, it should also be possible to limit the involvement of the armed forces in politics by playing "divide and rule" among the several armed services. There are some partial examples of use of this technique, without however substantial evidences of success. In most of the Latin American countries, of course, the army is by far the major armed service, and usually the only one in a position to play a significant political role. Chile's unusual geography, which gives her 2600 miles of coastline to only 296,000 square miles of territory, has made her navy the principal military arm. In fact, in the Chilean civil war of 1891, the Congress, supported by the navy, defeated President Balmaceda, who had the army fighting for him. Argentina and Brazil also have substantial naval forces, and officers of the Argentine Navy were prominent in the opposition to Perón, Admiral Isaac Rojas serving as Vice-President in both provisional governments following Perón's ouster. In fact, the *coup de grâce* was administered to Perón by the navy's threat to bombard Buenos Aires unless he resign. Some elements in the Venezuelan navy (as well as in the air force) took a hand in the movement that culminated in the overthrow of Pérez Jiménez, and an admiral, Wolfgang Larrazábal, became Provisional President of the caretaker government.

There are commonly differences in political orientation among the leadership of the different armed services; in general, one can say that the officer corps of the Latin American navies tend to have more democratic leanings than do the officers of the armies of the area. Of course, naval forces are not put in the position of performing internal policing duties, so do not have the army's corporate interest in the preservation of internal order. In addition, the foreign naval training missions in the area have long been those of the United States; naval officers often go to the United States itself for part of their training, and their professional models are the services of the United States and Great Britain. The training of many of the senior army officers, on the other hand, still goes back to the days in which German military missions and officers' schools were popular.[7] Doubtless, a certain amount of ideology was imbibed along with the professional training.

In recent years, the new air forces in the area have begun to play a political role. The Dominican air force, for example, which had been built up considerably during the Trujillo dictatorship, took a key part in the maneuvering that followed the assassination of the

[7] A German general served as chief of the Chilean General staff before and after the civil war of 1891, and the Bolivian army in the Chaco War (1933-38) was commanded, in the initial stages, by a German officer.

dictator, the ranking air force general becoming for a time Armed Forces Commander-in-Chief. The air force of Ecuador actually forced the army to back down and accept Vice-President Carlos Julio Arosemena Monroy as President after the deposition of President Velasco Ibarra in the fall of 1961, by attacking the Congressional chambers, where Arosemena was being held prisoner.

Although such incidents provide evidence that the navy and the air force may be able to bring power to bear in a political showdown, for normal political purposes they remain imperfect political instruments by comparison with the army.

A technique for insuring against hostile military intervention which has been tried without apparent success in Latin America (although it may have helped Hitler, who used it), is to attempt to gain a subjective commitment to the regime from the military by requiring the oath of allegiance to be taken to the dictator personally, rather than to the fatherland; and by giving compulsory courses of indoctrination in the ideology of the regime. Perón may have strengthened his position among the enlisted men in this fashion, although the opposition of naval officers to his regime was undoubtedly heightened by aversion to the personal oath and the indoctrination sessions required of them. The armed forces of democracies also have their oaths of allegiance and their indoctrination programs, of course, likewise of dubious efficacy.

Finally, there are administrative techniques of attempting to forestall military intervention in politics, which governments of Mexico since the Revolution have developed to a fine art. There is the frequent rotation of commands, so that a disgruntled general will not be able to gain sufficient control over his subordinates, nor establish relations of confidence with them adequate to lead them into a subversive enterprise. Promotion lists can be screened, of course, so that the loyal are rewarded and the potentially disloyal retired from the service prematurely. If the would-be conspirator has already become too strong to separate from the service directly, then, depending on his rank, he can be posted abroad as military attaché to an Embassy, sent around the world on some superfluous mission, or "promoted" to a seat in the cabinet at the head of one of the non-military departments, to remove him from a position of military command, isolate him from his followers, and gain time to prepare his downfall. An unscrupulous government can deliberately throw opportunities for large-scale graft in his way, in addition, either to take the bite out of his dissatisfaction with the *status quo,* or alternatively so as to be able to expose him subsequently and discredit him with his followers.

THE TYPES OF POLITICAL VIOLENCE

Discussions of politics normally confine themselves to the politics of stability: the maneuverings that occur when all sides accept the political institutions existing and work within and around them by peaceful means. In Latin America, perhaps because there exists a "legitimacy vacuum" of the type discussed above, politics frequently spills over the bounds of legality and operates outside them, taking the forms of what we might call a "politics of violence." The present section will discuss this type of politics.

Some possible techniques of eliminating the military from political activity were just discussed. Techniques of this type are applicable, by and large, when the military is in politics because it *wants* to be. It may also be the case, however, that circumstances draw the army into the political arena, whether it wants to be there or not. If this is in fact the situation, then it is pointless to try to neutralize the army by piecemeal techniques.

The army is necessarily involved in politics where there is a standing expectation of violence and where the use of violence is frequent and must be anticipated. Under these circumstances—for example, during the current term of President Betancourt in Venezuela and the recent one of President Frondizi in Argentina, where the life of each of the two governments had been threatened by violence, on the average, every other month—then the government needs continually to depend on the army to keep itself in power by crushing the attempts against it. The army, for its part, finds itself being used as a political tool to maintain a government in office by suppressing the opposition; it finds itself acting against some political groups on behalf of others; and the senior officers inevitably ask themselves if this is the role they wish to play. They may decide, as they have decided in Venezuela up to the time of writing, that it is their duty to support the incumbent constitutional government; but the temptation to stipulate conditions for their continued support will prove virtually irresistible, and the army will come to play the role described above as that of the "veto group." In other words, the government is put under the constraint of having to consider the views of the senior military leaders, and often of modifying policy consistent with their wishes, either expressed or anticipated.

On the other hand, an army that is being used to maintain a regime in power may rebel against the use to which it is being put, and either turn out the government itself,[8] or, like the Guatemalan army at the time of the Castillo Armas invasion against the Arbenz government described above, assume a "neutral" position and allow the government to be overthrown.

It should not be assumed, from the foregoing discussion, that the armed forces always hold the key to the outcome of situations of conflict—nor, for that matter, that all resorts to violence entail the use of organized military force as such. For purposes of clarity, let us posit the existence of a continuum of types of political action ranging from the peaceful and law-abiding expression of opinion in a public speech, say, all the way to civil war to the death. Then, many forms of political action only part of the way along the scale are common in the political life of Latin America, and in fact the overwhelming proportion of uses of force for political purposes are less than total. Let us review the most common types of "direct action," action outside constitutional channels, proceeding from the less to the more violent ends of the scale.[9]

[8] Colonel Nasser, in his book *The Philosophy of the Revolution,* explains the Egyptian army's overthrow of the monarchy in these terms.

[9] The creation of a single scale here is an unfortunately unavoidable over-simplification, since besides the level of violence used, other dimensions are relevant: the extent of the violence, in area or number of people involved, for example, or the magnitude of the stakes for which violence is used.

At the head of the direct action scale, one would have to set (1) *the mere threat of violence,* which may achieve the intended effect by itself. This may consist of no more than a statement of disapproval, public or private, of a given policy, say, together with the hint that, if necessary, disapproval may take a more concrete form. For example, the ranking general may announce something like "The armed forces direct me to express the gravest doubts about the wisdom of the policy with respect to *x* followed by His Excellency the Constitutional President of the Republic, and feel constrained to make clear that in the event of widespread public disorders attendant upon the final adoption of that policy, the armed forces cannot answer for the safety of the government"—the latter part of the statement being a hint that the army will connive at a *coup d'état* if need be. Or, of course, the threat may be more open and direct.

Different varieties of what are called in Latin America (2) *manifestaciones,* public demonstrations, rallies, parades, and the like, constitute a further stage along the road of violence, although a wide range of types of activity can be grouped under this head. Such demonstrations may pass off without further incident—everyone may go home quietly after the speeches are made, the slogans shouted, and enthusiasm for the cause built up. The justification for calling a peaceful demonstration of this kind a form of violent direct action is that the intended result is generally that of a show of strength—in effect, a kind of threat, as much as if to say: "Here we are, numerous, well-disciplined, enthusiastic; today we merely assemble peacefully; but if you do not adopt the policy we urge, we may not be so peaceable next time."

Of course, demonstrations frequently do not end without further incident, but develop instead into (3) *isolated acts of violence.* Buses and cars are stopped, overturned, smashed, burned; the houses and shops of members of opposing groups are stoned, broken into, looted. The forces entrusted with the maintenance of public order, for their part, are not standing idly by, and the forcible dispersal of public demonstrations of opposition forces is extremely common in Latin America—especially, of course, when the crowd becomes a violent mob and heads for the Presidential Palace; but not infrequently when the demonstration has been perfectly peaceable. Many dictatorships could find the turning-point in the train of events that led to their downfall in the public indignation following the death of some participant in a peaceful demonstration on which the police had opened fire. Actually, in several of the republics the police force in the capital includes riot squads trained and equipped for the dispersal of crowds without the use of firearms—with waterhoses, for example, or by tear gas; but all too often lives are lost unnecessarily—and with adverse political repercussions—by excess of zeal, or more likely of nervousness, on the part of the police.

(4) *The strike* should also be listed here, because it commonly has political aims, in contrast to its normal limited use for economic purposes in the United States. Its use becomes political, in Latin America, even where its goals are those of improvements in wages, hours, or conditions of work, because government intervention in labor disputes is so widespread, and so expected, that the desired outcome of a labor dispute will entail favorable government action in any case. In addition, unions also regularly use the strike weapon to influence government policy on questions other than those directly relating to labor.

On the other hand, the use of the strike for political ends has spread to groups other than organized labor. A strike by shopkeepers in Port-au-Prince in 1956 forced President Magloire from office, for example; a strike of professional men and women occasioned the downfall of Carlos Ibáñez del Campo, the dictator of Chile, in 1931; and a physicians' strike forced the resignation of the Salvadorean dictator Hernández Martínez in 1944.

Sporadic and isolated acts of violence were discussed above in connection with political demonstrations. Different in kind from them are the systematically planned individual acts of violence that go by the name of (5) *terrorism.* A terrorist campaign of assassinations and bombings, like the other types of act described above, may have the intention of directly inducing either a change in policy, or a change in government. It may also have the same effect indirectly, however, in that by forcing the government to become increasingly repressive in the all but impossible attempt to end terrorist attacks, it brings indifferent or apathetic public opinion increasingly over to the opposition. This was certainly the effect, probably intended, of the decision by Fidel Castro's movement to use terrorist tactics against the Batista dictatorship, which had until that time been relatively mild compared with what it later became, and which had been tolerated by large segments of the public that were rapidly alienated as the regime became more and more repressive in response to the *fidelista* campaign of terror.

Directly and immediately aiming at a change in government, of course, is the (6) *golpe,*[10] the forcible removal of the top political leadership from the seats of power, and their replacement by the leaders of the revolt. The classical Latin American "revolution" is of this uncomplicated type, and still occurs in this form, especially in the smaller countries, though no longer so frequently as formerly. Typically, the "palace revolt" of this type is engineered by a segment of the upper levels of command in the armed forces, involves little or no actual fighting, and is heard of by the public for the first time when the leadership of the revolt, now the "Provisional Government" or the "Patriotic Junta," announces the change over the radio and urges the citizens to remain calm and go about their normal business. Under the etiquette of the old-style *golpe,* the outgoing President and his colleagues would be permitted to go into exile, their departure facilitated and escorted. The extent of the military action accompanying the *coup* would be the deployment of a couple of platoons of men around the Presidential Palace, perhaps the Legislative Palace, and probably the radio stations (to prevent loyalists from broadcasting an appeal for support). If the *coup* is properly prepared, and the element of surprise preserved, the

[10] In English, *coup d'état!*

President has no opportunity to do anything else but yield, and relinquish his post.

In the case of what we may call the (7) *pronunciamento,* more people are involved, the power play occurs in public view, and the incumbent President has alternative actions among which he may choose. In a *pronunciamento,* a body of people—a section of the armed forces, a party, the people of a state or province—"pronounce" against the regime; that is, they openly raise the standard of revolt. After this has occurred, various consequences are possible: the rebels may march on the capital, gathering support on the way, there or near there to fight a decisive pitched battle against the adherents of the regime. The incumbents, on the other hand, may take a quick survey of the strength of the forces aligned on either side, and decide to retire into exile without pressing the issue to a trial of arms; perhaps all that is necessary is to sound out the leadership of the armed forces to determine whether it is prepared to fight the rebels or not, in order for the President to gauge which alternative to choose. And so it may be sufficient for an opposition leader to "pronounce" against the government, and then sit back and wait for it to fall.

Of course, the result may equally well go against him; those he thought would follow him in "pronouncing" may instead protest their loyalty; the armed forces may prepare to take to the field; and he may have to go into exile himself, or face capture and imprisonment. The *pronunciamento,* then, can eventuate in different ways —in a transfer of power attended with hardly more violence or public disturbance than the tradition *golpe;* or in protracted fighting that develops into actual (8) *civil war.*

A revolt of the *pronunciamento* type originating with a single barracks is known as the *cuartelazo (cuartel =* barracks). This may approach very close to the *golpe,* in that the showdown may occur entirely within the military, civilians playing only the role of bystanders, while the transfer of power takes place speedily and the action is localized. On the other hand, it clearly differs from the *golpe* in that the revolt occurs outside the circle of those having immediate access to the President, who is then left with a choice of alternative actions, to resist or not; while the rebels are prepared to fight if necessary.

MEETING THE THREAT OF VIOLENCE

What should be noted about the uses of violence referred to above is that it may be sufficient, and usually will be, merely to possess force and be prepared to use it; the necessity of actually shedding blood need not arise. The adversary may calculate the relative strengths of the two sides and decide to yield without bringing the issue to a hopeless trial of strength. Or he may not have the nerve, or the stomach, or the indifference to the loss of life, necessary to settle the contest by violence. This means, in effect, that a showdown over the control of the government or even over the direction of policy, where the threat of the use of force is involved, is in part a contest of wills. That is, an advantage lies with the more determined adversary—the one who is the more prepared to raise the level of violence. The adversary who shrinks from the use of violence is at a disadvantage in the struggle; he will be under pressure to yield rather than stand his ground and prepare for a physical conflict. In other words, the threat to use force may prove, where countered by an opposing willingness to use force, no more than a bluff.

Of course it takes courage, and a confidence in the eventual outcome of the dispute, to call a bluff of this kind. One reason to have confidence in a favorable outcome is the assurance of preponderant popular support; so that if the issue were to be pushed even to the point of civil war, the balance of forces would be favorable. Conversely, a bluff is more likely to collapse when the bluffer can be confronted with the threat to expand the theatre of conflict, and realizes that if this happens, his forces will be defeated by the opposition of the masses of the people.

One meaning of the foregoing is that a determined civilian government that has popular support can defy a military ultimatum to resign. That is, since it is possible for a popular cause to defeat a regular army in civil war—it has been done, as was mentioned above, in Cuba, Bolivia, and Costa Rica, in recent years—the military leaders may therefore be reluctant to follow through on an ultimatum that has been defied.

This was recently the case in Brazil, when the leaders of all three armed services announced that they would not accept as President, João Goulart, who as Vice-President was constitutionally entitled to succeed to the office from which Jânio Quadros had just resigned. However, when they were made to realize by the steadfastness of the Goulart forces that their position could only be maintained by the successful prosecution of a civil war, the military leaders retreated and accepted the inauguration of Goulart. Of course, all three military ministers were subsequently retired from the service by President Goulart. It had been made clear that the forces favoring the inauguration of Goulart would not accept the ultimatum of Marshal Denys and the other senior military leaders in several ways: some subordinate commanders announced that thenceforth they would take orders only from Goulart as constitutional President; one after another, leading political figures announced their adherence to the principles of succession provided in the constitution; and the governor of Goulart's home state of Rio Grande do Sul (who happened also to be Goulart's brother-in-law) mobilized his supporters in the state in preparation for civil war—an action reminiscent of the *pronunciamento* that originally brought Getúlio Vargas of Rio Grande do Sul, the great *caudillo* who had been Goulart's mentor, to the Presidency 31 years before, charging that the Presidential elections had been rigged against him.

Given circumstances of this type, there are several reasons why the leaders of an army enjoying an apparent position of preponderant strength may back down on an ultimatum they have given rather than carry it through, where that means actual fighting. As a rule, armies prefer to avoid fighting in any case; especially so when this involves fighting against compatriots. This reluctance will be strengthened, on the part of the army leadership, by the fact that although they have spoken in the name of the entire army in their political intervention, in actuality many subordinate commanders would not be prepared to follow their lead into combat against the legally constituted civilian authorities. In an actual trial of strength, the political generals at the top can guess that they will not be able to count on the continued loyalty to them of lower-ranking officers actually commanding troops. And yet even if the chain of command holds, and the army *in toto* takes to the field against organized civilian groups supporting the government, a popular government can count on widespread desertion among the enlisted men, reluctant to fire on friends and neighbors fighting in a cause with which they probably sympathize. This possibility, too, must be present in the mind of the general preparing to force his will on a recalcitrant government.

And so popular support itself constitutes a reservoir of strength on which a government can draw to withstand a military threat. A particularly striking demonstration of this thesis is given by the history of the development of stability in the government of Mexico over the last 40 years.

Until Porfirio Díaz had instituted his iron dictatorship in the last quarter of the nineteenth century, Mexican political history had run in the stereotyped channels of successful insurrection, dictatorship, crisis over succession to the Presidency, and further insurrection. After Díaz was overthrown by the Revolution of 1910, it seemed as if the old pattern would be revived. Venustiano Carranza managed to impose his authority over the other Revolutionary leaders and make himself President, only to be confronted, toward the end of his term, with a succession crisis and a successful revolt led by the man who felt he should have been picked as the government's Presidential candidate, but had not been: Álvaro Obregón. In classic fashion,[11] when Obregón's choice to succeed himself as President became known (it was Plutarco Elías Calles), the disappointed rival candidate, Adolfo de la Huerta, "pronounced" against the regime and began to gather an army.

According to all the precedents, the revolt was bound to succeed;

[11] The dynamics of the classic succession crisis are depicted masterfully by Martin Luis Guznán in his novel *La Sombra del Caudillo.*

leading Revolutionary generals went over to the revolt, being joined
in insurrection by probably the greater part of the army. In the
past, the people had almost automatically sided with the "outs" on
the premise that things couldn't get worse and might even get better.
But this revolt was different. The difference was that this time the
people had something to lose if the revolt succeeded; during his
term Obregón had fostered union organization and promoted social
legislation, as well as starting to implement the Revolution's program of land reform. Not only did this revolt collapse, but subsequent "election time" revolts became progressively feebler until by
1940 the defeated candidate fulminated and threatened, but refrained
from raising the standard of revolt. Since then Presidential elections
have no longer meant civil war in Mexico. This atrophy of the habit
of revolution is directly traceable to the reform measures which
ensured that, on the whole, the major organized interests of the
country would have an interest in the preservation of the *status quo*
that would lead them to fight, if need be, on the side of the constitutional authorities. In this sense one can say that although no
regime's tenure is absolutely assured, the best guarantee of continuance in office is broad popular support.

TRUE REVOLUTIONS

Perhaps at this juncture one should pause to make the point—
de rigeur in studies of Latin American politics—that the violent
changes of political control which occur so frequently in the region
and generally pass for revolutions, can hardly be called "revolutions" in the strict sense of an overturn of society and polity, since
the changes that occur have often consisted of no more than the
substitution of one group of individuals for another without far-
reaching consequences for the society. To earn the title of "revolution," a shift in the locus of power should be more than a palace
revolt with the ruling circle, or a *cuartelazo*. It is often said that the
revolution proper involves a restructuring of society and politics, a
re-shuffling of the class system. This is of course true, and in this
sense there can be "peaceful revolutions," just as much as there can

be violent shifts of power that are not revolutions. In fact, the genuine revolutionary process, the re-making of society, is likely to extend over a considerable period of time. In official parlance in Mexico, the Mexican Revolution that began in 1910 is regarded as still continuing.

Now the changes that collectively constitute the revolutionary process do not occur at random; they aim at fulfilling the goals of the revolution, at giving its ideals concrete embodiment in new institutions and patterns of behavior. If this is so, then the distinctive feature of a revolution is that it establishes new goals for the society; it reorganizes society, but it must first reorganize the values which that society accepts; a successful revolution means the acceptance as "good" of things that were not regarded as good before, the rejection as "bad" of things previously acceptable or commendable.

This transformation of the accepted value system can clearly be seen if one looks again at the example just cited above, the Mexican Revolution of 1910, one of the few genuine revolutions in Latin America. Prior to the Revolution, the Indian was semi-officially regarded as an inferior being, to be kept out of sight as much as possible, being prohibited by Porfirio Díaz's police from entering the Alameda, the public park in the center of Mexico City, for example. After the Revolution, Mexico's Indian heritage became a matter of national pride, to be stressed in her art and her history, to be studied at length in her universities, and the Indian himself became a subject of special government attention and expenditure. Prior to the Revolution, foreign investment was to be favored, nurtured, and protected, as one of the cardinal principles of national policy. After the Revolution, the presumption was to be against foreign investment, its role in the economy to be limited progressively to a demonstrably necessary minimum.

If the revolutionary process consists of the progressive implementation in practice of the new ideals posited by the revolution, then it is quite possible that not all the changes that occur will have been envisaged specifically by the original leadership. It is even true, moreover, that the ideals that the revolution comes to have will not be limited to those espoused by the original leaders of the revolution. In the revolutionary process, ideas which were "in the air," which were ripe for official acceptance, which embody genuine popular aspirations, will attach themselves to the ideology of the revolution, which in retrospect will have become something more than, although not opposed to, what the original leaders of the revolution contemplated. The initiator of the Mexican Revolution, Francisco I. Madero, for example, limited his demands to political reform—"Effective Suffrage; No Re-Election" in the motto that remains the official slogan of the Revolution to this day—whereas in retrospect the major achievements of the Revolution include, as well as the political reform, the reform of the landholding system, the establishment of unions, the incorporation of the Indian into national life, and the initiation of industrialization.

A clearer case, from our own day, of the autonomy of the revolutionary process once started in motion is that of the Bolivian Revolution of 1952. Neither of the two major structural changes wrought by the Revolution to date, the land reform and the nationalization of the tin mines, was deliberately initiated by the leadership of the National Revolutionary Movement that the revolution brought to power, although both measures were quite in keeping with MNR doctrine. The peasants seized the land, and the tin workers seized the mines; the government was left to establish a basis of legality for the *faits accomplis*.

One would probably be justified, accordingly, in concluding that the authentic revolutions that occur in Latin America in the present era, although they may take place under a variety of auspices and exhibit national peculiarities, if they are to succeed and establish themselves permanently, will embody the political values generally accepted today as legitimate: the legal equality of persons, the universal right to participate through representatives in political decision-making, and the individual's claim on his government for social justice. Not all of the Latin American countries have political orders that recognize these principles in practice; by peaceful or

violent means, revolutions that embody these principles will come
to them.

E. PARTIES AND PARTY SYSTEMS

THE DIMENSIONS OF PARTY

Politics is everywhere party politics. It is hard to imagine in what
way representative government could have any meaning without
political parties. Parties enable the voter to choose among intelligible alternatives. They develop and bring forward candidates to
fill offices in the gift of the people. At their best, they unite political
officials scattered among different branches of government in the
concerted attempt to effect a political program.

Accordingly, parties can be described in terms of three major
characteristics: the party's program, and the general principles from
which that program purports to be derived, the party ideology; the
social groups from which the party draws its electoral support, and
those from which its leaders come; and, less important, the chief
features of the internal organization of the party. The actions of
party leaders, however, will depend not only on these attributes
peculiar to the individual party, but also on the environment in
which the party operates, the whole political system. Necessarily,
this environment includes the whole range of factors discussed in
this book: political culture, social structure, and governmental structure. But it includes in addition two factors that may especially
appropriately be considered along with the parties themselves: party
systems, and electoral systems.

This section will deal, then, with the major factors, both intrinsic and extrinsic, which together determine party acts, taking
up first the combined dimension of ideology and social sources of
support.

PARTY TYPES, BY IDEOLOGY

In general, as one locates parties along a scale from Right to Left,
from conservative to radical, from supporters of the *status quo* to

innovators, one is also proceeding down the social ladder so far as the category into which the supporters of each party fall is concerned. In other words, the more conservative the party, the more likely its supporters are to be of high social status. This is of course to be expected, since those who resist change can be expected to be those who have most to lose by change. The assumption here is that a major determinant of political choice is the individual's class (that is, usually, economic) interest, and this is on the whole a sound assumption. In actuality, the individual normally—where the same parties continue to exist over time—inherits his party affiliation in Latin America just as in the United States; but he also inherits his class status, so the two continue in harmony in the typical case.

The assumption that individual social and economic interest determines party choice, although true in general, is not invariably valid; one could multiply examples of people who "should" support parties other than those they do. Nevertheless, the original assumption is accurate enough to serve as the basis for the discussion of the major varieties of party taken up in the following paragraphs.

These varieties are treated as separate parties, although in some countries, depending on the nature of the party system, they may exist as tendencies within larger, more inclusive, parties, or alternatively as coalitions of splinter groups in a fragmented system. No single country has parties representing the entire range of political tendencies listed below, although Chile comes close.

The Conservatives. Traditional Conservative parties, under various names, exist in perhaps half of the republics. They date, of course, from the earliest days of Independence, and, in a sense, even earlier. Essentially, the Conservatives represent the highest-status groups, the social elite, reproducing at their core the alliance of large landowners, high prelacy, and topmost echelon of military command that ruled during colonial times.

Today, however, members of families that still call themselves Conservative or remain loyal to Conservative parties may be involved in modern business activities and no longer dependent on an income from land ownership; their ideas may no longer be those

appropriate to the *ancien régime.* In fact, Latin American Conservatives, faced with the challenges of the modern world, have reacted
in three different ways: probably the major part of Conservatism
chooses to stand pat in its traditional position, denying any necessity
for change and steadily losing touch with political reality; a moderate wing of Conservative thought has accepted the need to change,
although attempting to control it, limit it, and slow it down, preserving as much as possible of the *status quo;* while a third segment
has reacted violently, taking an extreme position and resorting to
force and fraud in the attempt to maintain the traditional social
order.

The central core of ideas of Latin American Conservatism may
fairly be summarized as follows. Society inevitably includes classes
of people of different abilities, sensibilities, and merit. People in the
lower classes (especially where they are predominantly Indian) have
baser feelings, could not appreciate the refinements of living enjoyed by the upper classes, and would not work unless their condition made it absolutely necessary. Society requires order, with
each abiding in his proper place: a doctrine properly taught by the
Church, which should be especially protected and encouraged by
the State, especially in its ministry to the lower classes. The social
order that should be maintained includes the present distribution
of property. Proposals involving the redistribution of property, such
as progressive taxation or land reform, are clearly inspired by international Communism and would destroy the fabric of organized society, challenge the Divine order in the world, and tend to the
obliteration of proper social distinctions. In any case, attempts at
social amelioration are doomed by the fact that the harsh realities
of life are unavoidable features of the human condition, which will
not yield to human exertions.

With views of this kind, it is evident that traditional Conservative parties can accept democracy only half-heartedly or with reservations, if at all. In fact, several Conservative parties have long-
established reputations as falsifiers of elections, this being often the
only method by which a Conservative party can win elections in

the age of democracy. Rigging elections was the policy of Argentine Conservatives until 1910 and then again from 1930 to 1942, and the Colombian Conservatives have been guilty of the same thing. The examples from Central America are legion, of course.

For similar reasons, some Conservative politicians have cooperated with military leaders in staging anti-democratic *coups*.

Normally, Conservative chances in honest national elections depend on the discovery of a charismatic personality who can win *despite* his identification with the party; the fragmentation of the opposition (thus Ponce Enríquez was elected Ecuadorean President in 1956 from a field of three major candidates with only about 35 per cent of the vote cast); or the formation of a coalition (for example, in Chile the Conservative party has been able to join with Liberals and Radicals to form a majority combination).

It was mentioned above that, around the central core of Conservative belief, divergent tendencies exist. On the Right extreme, Conservatism shades into fascism—for example, in the politics of Laureano Gómez, the vitriolic Colombian newspaper publisher, former President and dictator of his unhappy country. With Laureano, Conservatism becomes reactionary, espousing violence against adversaries, bitterly hostile to the United States, Hispanophile (that is, fond of Spain), and pro-Franco. The regime of General Uriburu, which took power in Argentina in 1930, also bore this general complexion.

Several minor political organizations outside the Conservative parties—none of them having today a chance of coming to power through peaceful means—must be identified as downright fascist. The major fascist movements of Latin America are—or were, since the vogue of fascism has long passed its peak—the *Sinarquistas* of Mexico; the *Integralistas* in Brazil, led by Plinio Salgado, who at his high point garnered 8% of the vote in a Presidential election; González von Marees' *Nacista* party in Chile, now defunct, although many former *Nacistas* are still active in Chilean politics; the *ARNE* of Ecuador; and the *Falange Socialista Boliviano,* which still attempts revolts periodically. In addition, many dictators in office have

organized parties which necessarily, because of their use of violence, their exaltation of the leader, and their hostility to civil freedom, have features that appear fascist; whether one calls these parties fascist or not depends on how broad a definition he wishes to
allow the term. As in all countries, the fascists of Latin America are
the mentally unbalanced, the misfits of all classes, from top to bottom of the social scale. The avowed fascists, to repeat, are outside
the Conservative fold, although they are often tolerated by Conservatives as people "who mean well, but go to extremes."

The moderate Conservatives—like the Ospinistas in Colombia, or
the followers of Manuel Prado in Peru—although sharing their
basic outlook on society with the other Conservative tendencies, take
the position that one must make concessions to the times—to bend
to the wind lest one break, as it were. These Conservatives support
constitutional government and accept democracy. They are on the
whole pro-United States and sided with the Allies during World
War II (the Laureanista type of Conservative supported the Axis,
as a rule). Most members of the *Partido de Acción Nacional* in
Mexico would fall into this category, along with the *Pradistas* and
Ospinistas already cited.

The recent political history of Nicaragua, Paraguay, and Honduras necessitates a special word about the Conservative parties in
those countries. The major part of the Paraguayan Conservative
party, the Colorados,[12] has been simply an annex to the strongarm
military regime presided over by General Stroessner. The Conservatives of Honduras, the Nationalist party, stood in a similar
relationship to the dictatorship of Carías Andino, the wing of the
party opposed to Carías subsequently becoming the *Movimiento
Reformista*. In Nicaragua, on the other hand, it is the National
Liberal party that has been a utensil of the Somoza dictatorship,
but the Conservatives, too, have split over the issue of collaboration
with the regime.

Liberals and Radicals.   The emergence of the various parties was

[12] Not to be confused with the Colorados in Uruguay.

discussed briefly as part of a retrospect on the development of political issues in Latin America. As was pointed out, the original party struggle in the years following Independence in most of the republics was between Conservatives and Liberals. As more and more groups were admitted to participation in the political process—always those a little further down the socioeconomic scale—new political tendencies came into prominence, except for the fascist groups previously discussed, always to the Left of the Liberal parties. In countries where strong forces (to be discussed) made for the continuation of the two-party system, these tendencies were absorbed by, or contained within, the Liberal party. Where influences conducive to the maintenance of the two-party system were weak or lacking, a multi-party system developed. The possible fates in store for the Liberal party, then, were the following: it could become, in time, the dominant party in a two-party system, containing within itself various social groups and political tendencies. This is what has happened in Uruguay, Colombia, Honduras, and (until recently) Ecuador, where the Liberal parties include not only a traditional moderate wing, but also more radical elements like those referred to below as *aprista*. Alternatively, the Liberals could disappear from the scene, being absorbed into the newer parties or going over to the Conservatives as the upper social groups coalesced against the newly emergent elements. Today, in fact, most of the republics have no Liberal party as such. Thirdly, the party could continue to exist, where conditions favored a multi-party system, but on the basis of a narrow range of support. This development has reached its maximum in Chile, where the Liberals are simply one of a half a dozen "major" parties. Support of the Liberal party of Chile has narrowed down to comprise today principally moderately progressive businessmen and managers of the type of the present President, Jorge Alessandri Rodríguez.

Traditionally, the Liberals have been open-minded toward change, urging the cause of individual freedom against the Conservatives' championship of the principle of order, and favoring the rights of parliament over executive prerogative and, usually, those of local autonomy against central control. The Liberal is customarily at least mildly anti-clerical.

The core of support for the tradional Liberal party came usually from groups which, while part of the social elite, were not predominantly dependent on income from large estates, but were connected with business and "progressive" professions—journalism, law, and university teaching. The "inclusive" Liberal parties cited above, those operating in two-party systems, have today, in addition, working-class support.

The Radical parties grew out of the Left side of the Liberals, as it were, appealing especially to lawyers, schoolteachers, and civil servants, and stressing in their programs the extension of the suffrage, honest elections, and anti-clericalism, the latter especially as it applied to the schools, typical issues being those of government aid to religious schools and religious instruction in public schools. In Argentina, the Radicals absorbed the Liberals, emerging as easily the country's major party in numbers of supporters from 1910 on. The party split in the 1920s and has again split in recent years, on the latter occasion into the Intransigent Radicals (UCRI), led by Arturo Frondizi, and the People's Radicals (UCRP), whose major figure is Ricardo Balbín. The two Radical parties are the major ones in Argentina, so long as the Peronists are outlawed. In Ecuador, the reverse was the case: the Liberals re-absorbed the Radicals. In Chile, the third country in which the Radicals as such have constituted a major party, the party remains today normally the largest in voters' support, and is, in any case, of crucial importance since it occupies a pivotal position in the party spectrum—comparable to the traditional role of the French Radical party—which enables it normally to ally with either Right or Left in a majority coalition.

The Civic Union that emerged in the Dominican Republic after the assassination of Trujillo bears a strong resemblance to the old Radical parties, and should perhaps be classified with them. It resembles the Radical parties in the breadth of its original support, which, as in Argentina, extended to virtually all the foes of dictatorship; in the professional men who lead it; and in its principal goals, the establishment of constitutional government and the organization of fair elections. The Dominican Civic Union differs from the Argentine and Chilean Radical parties, however, in that the outcome of party competition has not left it (like the Chilean party) the central group in the party spectrum, enabling it to rule but forcing it continually to choose between Left and Right alliances; nor (like the Argentine Radicals) the dominant party, but split by internal dissension. Instead, because of the vacuum to the Right caused by "detrujilloization," and the rise of a strong party to the Left, the *Partido Revolucionario Dominicano* of Juan Bosch, the Civic Union has been pushed into playing the role of the conservative party in the emergent Dominican party system.

Christian Democrats or Christian Socialists. The growth of the Christian Democrats as a distinctive category of political party is predominantly a phenomenon of the period since the end of World War II. Christian Democracy, or Christian Socialism, as it is sometimes known, is an attempt to combine loyalty to the Church, and support of its political claims—which, while varying from country to country in relation to the number of the devout and the traditions of each land, always include autonomy for church schools and the protection of religious instruction and worship—with a progressive position on social questions. That is, traditionally, in Latin America at least as much as in Europe, support for the Church has been identified with social conservatism. The doctrines of the Church affecting politics that were most emphasized were those elaborating the duties of obedience to secular authorities, which must be presumed to be ordained of God. Christian Democracy has chosen rather to stress those elements of Catholic doctrine that postulate the duty of all to be charitable in mutual relations, to acknowledge and respect the spiritual equality and the familial needs of all humankind. Specifically, this position finds its immediate authoritative support in the social encyclicals of Leo XIII (and now of John XXIII) and especially the *Rerum Novarum* and *Quadrege-*

simo Anno, which, although not as "socialist" as often supposed, do
acknowledge the necessity for minimum standards of life for workingmen, and point out that capitalism in itself does not satisfy the
requirements that Christianity demands of an economic system.

These views were not new in Catholic thought when announced
authoritatively, of course, but the stress placed on them at the time
constituted something of a departure from pre-existing practice. This
was still a long way from countenancing "Christian" political
parties, however, the position of the Church having normally been
that it did not care to be identified exclusively, even indirectly, with
any single political current, but would maintain good relations with
all political tendencies that did not clearly violate Christian norms
nor attack the necessary secular basis for religious worship and instruction. Accordingly, while small "Christian" political parties of
the Center and Center-Left were founded in the first three decades
of the century, in Uruguay and Chile (as they were in Italy and
France), these were barely tolerated by the Church hierarchy, and
never gained the stature of major parties in the inter-war period.

Christians in politics were drawn to the Left, however, during
the period of fascist dominance in Europe, when they found themselves cooperating, in the opposition or underground, with Liberals,
Socialists, and Communists. Something of the same effect was noticeable a little later in Argentina, Peru, and Venezuela, where similarly
broad-based cooperation, in the open, underground, or in exile, was
effected against the dictatorships of Perón (in its later stages), Odría,
and Pérez Jiménez, respectively. In the meantime the Church had
relaxed and—almost, but not quite—abandoned its reservations
about "Christian Socialist" parties, and parties were founded in Peru
and Argentina to join the now flourishing Christian Democratic
movements of Chile and Venezuela.

The status of the individual parties today is roughly as follows:
in Venezuela the Christian Social party (COPEI, after an earlier
name) is the second or third largest party in the country in the size
of its support, and has collaborated in recent years with its present
partner in the government coalition, *Acción Democrática.* In Chile,

the Christian Democrats (earlier the National Falange, not to be confused with the Spanish and Bolivian Falanges) are one of the major three or four parties in size of vote, have attracted much support among progressive intellectuals, and may well have a bright future. On the other hand, they are faced with serious difficulties in forming the coalitions that the nature of Chilean politics demands, despite their central position in the party spectrum. Immediately to the Right of the party stand the Radicals, whose anti-clerical tradition presumably makes a coalition with them out of the question. To the Left is the Socialist party, a highly desirable coalition partner since coalition with it would help compensate for the pull to the Right that the party always feels. The Socialist party is itself however in coalition with the Communists, thus demolishing the possibilities in that direction. Thus despite an able and popular leadership, headed by the dynamic Eduardo Frei, and a responsible and progressive program, future success of the Chilean Christian Democrats depends on only two possibilities: either the fragmentation of the Right, together with an attendant drop in the strength of the Radicals, will leave the Christian Democrats able to win a Presidential election on their own; or a split between the Socialists and their allies further to the Left will make a Socialist-Christian Democrat coalition possible.

The Christian Democrats in Peru, Argentina, and Uruguay (in Uruguay known as the *Unión Cívica*) are each currently about the fourth or fifth strongest parties in their respective countries; however, this means much less in terms of relative importance in Peru than it would in Chile; it means less in Argentina than in Peru; and in predominantly two-party Uruguay, it means hardly anything at all. Splinter parties bearing a "Christian Democratic" or "Social Christian" label have been founded also in Ecuador, Bolivia, and in several of the Central American republics in recent years, without amassing any appreciable support.

A problem faced by all the parties of Christian-Social orientation is that of maintaining equilibrium between the terms at the two ends of the hyphen, as it were, and especially of not allowing the

party's pro-clerical predilections to eclipse its stand for social progress. The problem arises in this form because many supporters are
attracted to an avowedly Christian party, for reasons of conscience,
who do not share its progressive orientation on social questions. The
more devout are still likely, in Latin America as elsewhere, to be
the more conservative; and the party's leaders have to maintain
constant vigilance lest the party's political position begin to drift
Rightward in response to opinion among the rank and file. The
Christian Democrats are particularly subject to the operation of
centrifugal ideological forces, since they draw support from all levels
of society, and all walks of life: organized labor, business, the professions, and agriculture. To be a "Christian Democrat" sounds and
feels more pleasant than to be a "Conservative," apparently, and
moderate Conservative parties frequently refer to themselves as
Christian Democrat—the PAN in Mexico, for example.

The Aprista Parties. In perhaps half of the republics there exist
parties of the moderate democratic Left that one could group loosely
as *aprista,* after the oldest and most prominent of the group, the
APRA (*Alianza Popular Revolucionaria Americana*) of Peru. Like
the Christian Democrats, these are parties of recent origin; unlike
all the parties listed heretofore, they fall outside the categories of
the traditional European party systems. Accordingly, some writers
have stressed their indigenous American character, although actually
parties comparable in program and sources of support have developed in recent years in Africa and Asia.

The impulse that animates the *aprista* parties might loosely be
termed "socialist" in the general sense in which the Christian Democrats are referred to as Christian Socialists; indeed, *aprista* leaders
often refer to themselves as "socialist." They differ clearly from the
Socialist parties proper, however, in being pragmatic, unbound by
doctrine, not committed to nationalization of economic enterprises
on principle, certainly not Marxist. *Aprista* parties in power have
shown themselves flexible and realistic, for example, encouraging or
controlling private economic enterprise as the needs of the economy

seemed to indicate, being prepared to cooperate with the United States if North American purposes seem worthy of support, and reaching accommodations with the Church without either favoritism or persecution. The voluminous writings of Haya de la Torre and his counterparts in other countries notwithstanding, what has guided *aprista* leaders has been not doctrine but general principles of sympathy with the underprivileged, the maintenance of political democracy, and national progress and development. In these respects one might compare parties of this type with the Democratic parties in the Northern United States.[13]

The social bases of the parties' support are principally to be found among organized labor; the organized peasantry; and intellectuals. The major parties that could probably be denominated as *aprista* in outlook and program are, of course, the APRA itself, in Peru; *Acción Democrática* in Venezuela; the *Febreristas* in Paraguay; the *Partido Revolucionario,* led by Mario Méndez Montenegro, in Guatemala; the *Partido Revolucionario Dominicano* in the Dominican Republic; the *Liberación Nacional* in Costa Rica; and possibly also the *Movimiento Nacional Revolucionario* in Bolivia and the Mexican *Partido Revolucionario Institucional,* although the special circumstances in which the latter two parties find themselves endow them with certain distinctive characteristics that will be discussed later. In addition, there are *aprista* elements within the area's Liberal and Radical parties.

Except for the parties in Paraguay and, perhaps, Guatemala, the *aprista* parties cited above are all either in power at present or else major contenders for power. Once in power, however, the parties' pragmatism and sense for realities have led to policies too moderate for the younger and more extreme members, who then secede to the Left. This has happened in recent years to *Acción Democrática* in Venezuela, and also to the APRA itself, which has not been in power but has supported a moderate conservative gov-

[13] Or perhaps more exactly with the ADA (Americans for Democratic Action).

ernment; a Left secession is a continuing possibility for *Liberación Nacional* in Costa Rica. These "secessionist" movements will be considered below in the section on Popular Socialist parties.

Just as there are Communist and Socialist "Internationals," *aprista* parties hold international meetings and maintain contact with each other, although in a less formal way. In addition, José Figueres, ex-President of Costa Rica and founder of the *Partido Liberación Nacional,* has started the Institute for Political Education, which offers a short course in economics, international relations, and practical political action for young future leaders of the parties of the democratic Left. The PLN also publishes a political journal, *Combate,* which is well-known in the hemisphere.

Socialist Parties. Socialist parties have been, on the whole, of almost as little political significance in Latin America as they have in the United States. With the exception of Chile, Socialist parties have never been able to entertain any realistic hope of coming to power by winning elections. Perhaps before one discusses the prospects of the Socialist parties in the Latin American republics, however, one should first make some fundamental distinctions about parties called "socialist," since the word has come to have varying meanings and certainly varying connotations.

The traditional Socialist parties of Latin America strongly resemble European Socialist parties, and indeed have flourished especially in the states of southern South America to which European immigrants came in great numbers during the second half of the nineteenth century, the major period of growth of the Socialist movement. These parties have been on the whole doctrinaire opponents of the capitalist system on principle, regardless of its performance as a producer of goods and services, and have been content with doctrinal purity and a small intellectual following, plus some working-class supporters. Their programs were not adapted to contemporary issues, but stressed instead a fundamental view of a desirable form of economy and society; issues of international relations were secondary by a long way. Perhaps Senator Alfredo Palacios of Argentina represents this classic type of Socialist at its grandest—a man high in public esteem, respected for his integrity, but without a chance of entering a government: not unlike Norman Thomas in the United States, although better known and rather more successful electorally!

Because of the fragmented nature of the party systems in Ecuador and Chile, individual Socialist party members have been Cabinet ministers in those countries under several Presidents, despite the limited following of the parties themselves. In addition, a handful of Socialist party representatives can be found in the national legislatures of Argentina, Brazil, and Uruguay.

Parties of a quite different type have recently been appearing, usually under the name "Popular Socialist." These parties, although they call for domestic social reform, are much more concerned with the international scene. In international relations, they support the positions taken by the Soviet Union, and today especially lay heavy stress on their sympathies with the government of Fidel Castro in Cuba. In domestic politics, they stand ready to cooperate with local Communist parties—indeed they enroll individual Communists as members—and they are prepared to countenance violence to achieve their objectives, if necessary. In this last respect they often do not differ markedly from some of the other Latin American parties, of course, but the contrast with the traditional Socialist parties is quite marked. A list of current "Popular Socialist" parties, or protoparties, would have to include the groups led by Vicente Lombardo Toledano in Mexico (the Popular Socialist Party) and Francisco Julião in Brazil (the Peasant Leagues of Resistance), the *Partido Revolucionario Abril y Mayo* in El Salvador, the *Partido de Unidad Revolucionaria* in Guatemala, the *Movimiento de Izquierda Revolucionaria* in Venezuela and Peru, Fidel Castro's own party, of course, currently the O.R.I., and groups elsewhere called *Frentes* (or *Movimientos*) *de Liberación Nacional*. In addition, there are Popular Socialist elements within several other Latin American parties and political movements, whose unhappy leaders have to try to prevent their organizations from disintegrating in the split between *Fidelista* and more moderate elements. Dissident wings have already, at the time of writing, split off from *aprista* parties and formed new groups over this and related issues; the *Movimiento de Izquierda Revolucionaria* (MIR) was formed from the youth movement of *Acción Democrática* in Venezuela, for example.

Popular Socialist parties are strongest among students, the city poor, and in some cases the peasants, although there is generally also some support from dissident union members. These are parties that do not seem likely today to come to power through the ballot, but in a revolutionary situation might be in a position to seize power, a possibility for which some of them prepare actively.

The only governing party of this type is found in Cuba. There it has put into effect a program resembling that of the Soviet Communist party—only more so. That is, it has gone farther faster than the Soviet Communist Party: in moving more swiftly into the "state farm" organization of agriculture, without a long "collective farm" stage (in Soviet theory, the state farm is regarded as a more advanced form of organization than the collective farm, which still retains individualistic elements); in renouncing elections, instead of at least going through the forms of an election process, as is done in the Soviet Union; in instituting statist forms of economic organization on a schedule of maximum acceleration, so far at least without the concessions to individualism (for example, the New Economic Policy, the relaxation after Stalin's "Dizzy with Success" speech, or Premier Khrushchev's decentralization program) that have marked the process within the Soviet Union.

A realistic appraisal of the Popular Socialist parties might well lead to the view that they are more "Left" than the Communists; that they represent, in fact, a kind of neo-Trotskyite position. This can be said because the Communist parties themselves, since their organization in their present form after the Bolshevik Revolution, have placed loyalty to the Soviet Union, as the "first Socialist state" and the leader of the world proletarian movement, ahead of other considerations. This primary loyalty to the Soviet Union has meant that the party line at any one time soft-pedals or abandons temporarily its long-term economic and political goals. Thus, during the period of the Popular Front in the 1930s, the main danger to the Soviet Union was that of aggressive Nazism and fascism, and other objectives were subordinated to the struggle against fascism. Accordingly, local Communist parties temporarily dropped attacks on the democratic parties, and rallied behind democratic leaders who opposed fascism in the international arena. Extreme revolutionary parties which, while cooperating on occasion with the international Communist movement, do not form part of it, are under no such compulsion to forgo their own domestic programs in the interest of the requirements of Soviet foreign policy. They can thus pursue a doggedly violent and revolutionary line with consistency, ignoring the twists and turns of Soviet policy to which loyal Communists must pay so much attention. An attitude of this kind is regarded by the Communists as "Left-wing dogmatism" and even Trotskyism, Trotsky himself having advocated the pursuit of a consistent "hard" policy of violent revolution.

It is clear therefore that in some ways a Popular Socialist movement may constitute a greater danger to the established constitutional order in any given country than the local Communist party itself, disciplined, dedicated, and supported by the Soviet Union though it may be. This is so because the allegiance to the Soviet Union that is the first principle of the local Communist party leads it to make sudden shifts of position in response to changes in Soviet policies that make its dependence on foreign guidance clear, and make it appear disloyal and even rather ridiculous. The classic example of this is of course the sudden shift away from an anti-Nazi position after the Hitler-Stalin pact, and then back again after the Nazi attack on the Soviet Union. Furthermore, the policies the local party follows, in accord with the current Soviet line, may be not at all adapted to local conditions, and may thus lead to a steady diminution in its local following. An autonomous Popular Socialist movement does not carry liabilities of this type, and parties of this character do in fact uniformly have greater followings than the Communists themselves, with the possible exception of Chile.

One of the distinctions between the "traditional" Socialist party and the new "Popular Socialist" movements is that the traditional Socialists were normally reluctant to cooperate with the Communists, and often were strongly anti-Communist, the Communists representing a perverted variety of socialism and being their rivals for working-class support; whereas the Popular Socialists, as we have seen, are pro-Communist and willing to cooperate with the local Communist party. A major exception to this general rule, however, can be found in Chile. There, almost continuously since 1936, the traditional Socialist party has been in coalition with the Communist party and some smaller left-wing groups in a "Popular Front" for electoral purposes.[14] The Chilean Socialist party is proportionately the strongest in the hemisphere, if one excepts the governing party of Cuba, and it shares control of the labor movement with the Communists. In this, as in other respects, Chilean and French politics strongly resemble each other.

Communist Parties. Latin American Communists loom larger in the consciousness of North Americans or of Right-wing Latin Americans than they do in reality. This is due in part to imprecision in political discourse; in part to ignorance; in part to the tactics of the Communist movement since Lenin's day of insinuating its members into non-Communist organizations, which they try to dominate and in whose name they try to act; and in large part to the fact that, since Communism is unpopular, unscrupulous politicians habitually call their liberal and Left-wing opponents "Communists" in order to discredit them. This is a favorite technique of dictators, of course, of such ancient standing and used by men who lie so continually that North Americans by now should really know enough to look beyond the name-calling to the facts—should, but often don't. In some cases, the instinctive reaction of the dictator and the Right-wing demagogue to call his democratic opponents "Communists" reaches really ludicrous extremes, as when the present President of

[14] The Radical party, which provided the Popular Front's Presidential candidates during most of its first ten years of existence—two of them successful—is no longer part of the grouping.

Haiti, François Duvalier, in November of 1960 actually expelled the Archbishop of Port-au-Prince, François Poirier, on charges of financing Communist activities.

One of the problems in trying to gauge correctly the extent of Communist strength in Latin America is that in almost all the re-publics the party is outlawed, either specifically by name, or under the terms of a general statute prohibiting parties that advocate violent revolution or that are controlled from abroad. At the time of writing the party is legal only in Chile, Uruguay, Venezuela, and of course Cuba. Where it is outlawed, it continues to operate as a political party anyhow if it can, either on its own under another name, or else within a "Popular Socialist" or "Labor" party. Even where it may operate legally, however, the party maintains a clandestine organization against the day when it may have to go underground.

Although the Right-wing dictator always makes a conspicuous display of his anti-Communism (especially if he is seeking economic aid from the United States), the Communists have actually been able to work out mutually satisfactory arrangements with ostensibly anti-Communist dictators; for example, in return for a free hand in infiltrating labor union leadership, they can offer freedom from "labor trouble" to the dictator. Among recent dictators, Fulgencio Batista is reputed to have had an arrangement of this kind with the Cuban Communists, even though the party was legally dissolved. Perón and Vargas, Ibáñez and Odría, have also found it possible to cooperate with local Communists on occasion. When the Commu-nists undertake this type of arrangement with a dictator, however, the standard procedure is to take out insurance by maintaining con-tact with the opposition, in exile or underground. What has hap-pened in such cases is that the party has ostensibly "split," one wing supporting, the other opposing, the regime, so that the party is well-connected whether the regime continues or is overthrown.

Where it meets with a regime receptive to its overtures, of course, the party endeavors to have loyal members appointed to official posi-tions, with the hope that some day it will be in a position to dominate the government. This policy was temporarily successful in Guatemala under the Presidency of Jacobo Arbenz Guzmán (1951-54), and has been a smashing success so far in Cuba under the regime led by Fidel Castro Ruz. By affording Fidel Castro a hard-working, conscientious cadre of men willing to give concrete effect to his vague revolutionary aspirations, and by "educating" Castro himself into seeing that his nebulous Leftist ideas could be made sense of in a Marxist framework, Communists were accepted into the Revolutionary government of Cuba, to attain, by the middle of 1961, the commanding position.

Today the party's strength, outside Cuba, is probably greatest in Chile, Brazil, and Venezuela. It is a minor political factor in Uruguay and Argentina, and has at least some intellectual influence in Peru, Mexico, Guatemala, and Panama. Elsewhere the party is without significance, so far as one can see at the present time. In Chile it is strongest among organized labor, in Venezuela among the city poor, in Brazil among the city poor at present and probably among the peasantry of the depressed Northeast states in the future.

Personalist and Caudillo *Parties.*   In Latin American political life, heavy stress is placed upon individual political leaders. Parties and political tendencies within parties are often known by the names of their leaders, even after these leaders have passed on. Sometimes the party bears the leader's name not as an informal soubriquet, but as the formal party title—for example, Perón's party was officially the *Partido Peronista,* that of Velasco Ibarra of Ecuador the *Federación Nacional Velasquista.*

To be sure, this phenomenon is not unknown outside of Latin America. The name of a well-known political figure often serves as a shorthand description of a political tendency in the United States, for example; one speaks of Taft or of Goldwater Republicans. However, there is a considerable difference between the designation of a party or political tendency by the name of an individual where this is used for purposes of identification and easy reference, and where its significance is that the party exists to put the leader in power.

and has no autonomous existence nor a specific program other than to endorse his views.

Political organizations of the latter type may be called personalist parties. They abound in Latin America (and in other areas that are at comparable stages of political development) especially, as we have already noted, because of the limited development of the political systems of the states of the area. Loyalties to persons fill the void left by the absence of continuing representative institutions or organizations that should command loyalty. Panama or, more strikingly, Haiti, provide classic examples of personalism of this type. In addition, loyalty to a commanding personality provides a cement holding together individuals for purposes of common political action where because of the rudimentary development of the country's "social technology," the organizational mechanisms that perform this function elsewhere are absent. In the unordered chaos of the country's political life, dominant individuals provide the only rallying points. This situation is total in at least the two countries cited; it invades the political systems elsewhere to varying extents, so that there may be one or two permanently organized, doctrinally sophisticated, modern political parties, competing with an array of personalist groupings. Indeed, it may be that any given political party is itself compounded of personalist and non-personalist factors in uneasy coexistence.

Personalism is especially a feature of the political life of the less advanced, less organized, smaller, poorer countries. When it emerges and develops to significant proportions in advanced societies, it can be taken as evidence of crisis and the breakdown of normal and stable political patterns, as the cases of the personalist attractiveness of Roosevelt in the United States, Churchill in Britain, and De Gaulle in France demonstrate. (One might almost say "Blessed is the country without great men; for its troubles are small.")

In the republics where effective political participation is confined to a small social class, the personalist party may be no more than a small clique gathered around some prominent political figure;

this is predominantly the case in Panama, for example. Alternatively, the personalist party may support the type of figure Rosendo A. Gomez has called the demagogic *caudillo,* the authoritarian personal leader who rules, or aspires to rule, not simply by force and fear, but with the aid of a mass popular following.

One can consider the *"caudillo* party" as a special category of party in an ideological spectrum because, by virtue of its personalism and its mobilization of mass support, a party of this kind *necessarily* has a distinctive type of ideology, or pseudo-ideology.

In recent years, the leading examples of the *caudillo* party have been the *Partido Peronista* in Argentina, the *Unión Nacional Odriísta* in Peru, the *Federación Nacional Velasquista* in Ecuador, Rojas Pinilla's *Alianza Nacional Popular* (ANAPO) in Colombia, Ibáñez del Campo's Farmer-Labor party in Chile, and the National Republican Party of Rafael Angel Calderón Guardia in Costa Rica. Generals Odría of Peru, Ibáñez of Chile, and Rojas Pinilla of Colombia, all of whom originally came to power by means of the military *coup,* only emerged as real demagogues after their departures from the President's chair, each trying to build up a popular following in the attempt to stage a comeback. One way to distinguish the classic military or paternalistic dictator from the demagogic *caudillo* is that the latter, once deposed, has the popular following to make an attempt at a comeback in a democratic election with a reasonable chance of success. Both Velasco and Ibáñez, cited above, succeeded in this feat, as did Getúlio Vargas of Brazil (of whom more later). Rojas, Odría, and Calderón have made the attempt, while Perón is deterred from it only by legal rulings against his candidacy.

The principal features of the *"caudillo* party's" ideology are the following. In the first place, since it aims to concentrate power in the hands of one man, it stresses the need for leadership and decries the slowness, the cumbersomeness, and the alleged injustice of constitutional forms. Then, since it attempts to build a mass following, the party necessarily promises—in however cloudy terms—social progress, improvement in the lot of the masses, and the uplifting of the downtrodden. Yet since the party is founded on the sheer desire to achieve power and build a following, the party's ideology and stated goals are simply the most appropriate weapons in the struggle; they are thus *ad hoc,* nebulous, lacking in content, and to be modified or abandoned if tactical requirements so indicate. The party is prepared to use violence, especially once in power— since the achievement and retention of power is the movement's prime *raison d'être.* Nor is it reluctant to preach a gospel of hate and aggression—against the well-to-do, the foreigner, and the movement's opponents. In sum, the ideology of the *"caudillo* party" is authoritarian, pseudo-socialist, nationalist, aggressive, eclectic.

The party thus presents many faces to the observer, and is likely to elude being placed in the traditional series of categories. Consider, for example, how some of the most able observers of the Latin American scene have characterized the movement led by Juan Perón. Robert J. Alexander has most recently classed Perón with the "Jacobin Left," which also includes Fidel Castro; and indeed in the demagoguery, the anti-Yankeeism, the championing of the dispossessed, there are clear resemblances between the Argentine and the Cuban. William W. Pierson and Federico G. Gil categorize Peronism, as an indigenous, nationalist, labor-oriented movement, with the *aprista* parties; and one can find similarities between the two, with the National Revolutionary movement in Bolivia serving as a sort of "missing link," especially in its early years, when it was directly influenced by Peronism, and was more prone to violence, and a great deal more anti-Yankee, than it has since become.

It used to go without saying that Perón was a fascist; and perhaps this is still the best category, in the lexicon of European politics, in which to place him. Clearly, Perón studied Mussolini's techniques at first hand while a military attaché in Italy; his demagoguery and use of force were quite fascist-like (again using "fascist" in its Italian denotation); and, like Mussolini, he raised insincerity and opportunism to a high principle—Perón said of his *Justicialismo* what Mussolini had written of fascism, that its essence was to be pragmatic, to meet each problem on its own terms, not with some predetermined set of solutions. Harold E. Davis has aptly compared Peronism with "other modern fascist-like regimes which have tried to clothe their naked quest for power with the respectable garments of an ideology." [15] Like Franco, to carry the parallel further, Perón was also fond of describing his position as a third one, "between" the mistaken poles of Communism and capitalism, thus making it appear moderate and reasonable. However, if there is one clear characteristic of the *"caudillo* party" and its leader, it is that they can always attract and work with extremists—national chauvinists, Communists, authoritarians: with all men of violence and hatred— never with liberals, moderates, democrats, constitutionalists.

There is a story that a Minister of the Interior told Curnonsky, the noted French epicure, that before approving him for the award of the Legion of Honor, he had checked his police dossier for "political reliability," and found not one, but two sets of records. Under "Curnonsky," which was a nom-de-plume, he found an account of the doings of an anarchist and Bolshevik of disorderly habits and disreputable associates; under the gourmet's real name were listed the activities of a reactionary and active Royalist, who regularly dined with the Count of Paris, the pretender to the throne. "Well," the minister told him, "I averaged the two and decided you were a loyal republican." The same effect is often visible in appraisals of the *caudillo* party; the observer averages its Right and Left supporters, the reactionaries and the radicals, the military authoritarians and the haranguers of street crowds, and concludes that it must be a "center" grouping. This has been the burden of much of the discussion of the followers of Ibáñez in Chile, of Velasco Ibarra in Ecuador, of Calderón Guardia in Costa Rica, for example, all of whom have been supported at one time or another by both conservative nationalists and Communists. The demagogic *caudillo* attracts supporters from both extremes of the spectrum because, although he speaks to the mobs in the words they wish to hear, con-

[15] Harold E. Davis, ed., *Government and Politics in Latin America* (Ronald, New York, 1958), p. 112.

servative authoritarians can hope that he will provide the "strong hand" that will discipline the people to obedience.[16]

When in power the *caudillo's* policies may even continue to satisfy both elements, though commonly those at one extreme (the dynamics of governing being what they are, it is usually the Left) complain about the leader's having been captured, or having sold out.

This ambiguity in the demagogic *caudillo's* attractive power to these two forces—authority and poverty—comes through quite clearly in the case of Getúlio Vargas of Brazil, although Vargas did without the harshness and needless cruelty that characterize the dictators of the Hispanic countries, and was supported by moderates as well as extremists. Vargas was able to rule the country well enough without an organized party, on a personal basis; parties have been relatively unimportant in Brazilian politics, in any case. When Vargas, who was always the height of flexibility, decided at the end of World War II that democracy was back in fashion, and prepared to get himself confirmed in the Presidency by election, he organized a political party, the Social Democrats, out of his administrative appointees in the state governments; this is now a conservative party, if one can give Brazilian parties ideological labels. Shortly thereafter, the dictator was deposed by a military *coup,* and prepared a comeback by organizing as an appropriate vehicle the Brazilian Labor Party, based on the labor movement, which had benefited from legislation adopted during his term. Originally, Vargas had intended to organize officeholders and unionists into a single party, but had been dissuaded by an advisor on the basis that the two elements would be incompatible, and nothing would be lost by creating two parties rather than one.

PARTY SYSTEMS AND ELECTORAL SYSTEMS

We have looked so far at the internal determinants of a party's behavior—its ideology and the social forces it represents. But the party's actions are also shaped by the environment in which it must

[16] A similar pattern was visible in Hitler's following.

operate: the organization of the government that it seeks to control, of course, but also the nature of its competition—the other parties—and the rules that determine success or failure in the party battle—the electoral system. Since the party system and the electoral system in each country are closely related, they will be discussed together. Before getting into the detailed discussion, however, let us first glance briefly at one of the leading theoretical questions in empirical political science, that of the causal relation between party system and electoral system.

What determines whether a country will have a system in which two major parties compete, or one in which a half-dozen "medium-sized" groups contend for power?[17] The answer that probably the majority of students of the problem would give is that the crucial determinant is the electoral system; if representatives are elected in "single-member districts," that is, where there is to be only one victor in the election, then the various groups will tend to coalesce into only two parties; otherwise, a multi-party system is to be expected. This is so, runs the argument, since in a single-member election the victor needs to garner at least 50% + 1 of the available votes. Clearly, no more than two parties can have a reasonable expectation of reaching this figure. Accordingly, third, fourth, and so on parties, realizing the hopelessness of their cause, will join with the major party they consider the lesser evil and try to realize their goals from within it. Where representatives are elected in multi-member districts, however, the chances of the lesser parties are not hopeless at all; they may elect a few representatives whose legislative votes will be valuable for bargaining purposes, and may even hope to hold a balance of power. For example: under perfect proportional representation (or as perfect as it can be without dividing legislators into fractions!) over the whole country—say, the current Israeli electoral system—then a party garnering 7 per cent of the vote will take just 7 per cent of the seats in the legislative assembly. That 7 per cent

---

[17] Here and throughout, the number of parties considered to be active in the party system will include only those groups that can entertain serious expectations of being able to gain power and not the miniscule groups, to be found everywhere, which are taken seriously by no one but themselves.

may be crucial in making up a government majority, and the party can expect to be able to exact a price, in concessions on policy questions, and in office for party leaders, in return for its support. In electoral systems based upon proportional representation principles, accordingly, there is no reason for the smaller parties to go out of business and merge with a larger group—in fact there is every reason not to.

Various objections can be raised to this thesis. It presupposes, of course, that party leaders and voters act rationally and will not continue to "waste" their efforts in a hopeless cause. Although this is on the whole a sound assumption, exceptions to it certainly exist. More interesting is the objection raised, among others, by Leslie Lipson, that the electoral system does not after all create itself, but is set up by a party or coalition of parties—normally in the expectation that its provisions will redound to the benefit of the groups that framed it. In other words, the party system may well antedate the electoral system, and may determine *it,* rather than the other way around. This in fact is probably what has happened in most countries. It is, however, solely of historical interest and in no way eliminates the causal relation between electoral system and party system that was just described, but on the contrary assumes it; if the parties are interested in modifying the electoral laws in their interest, then clearly those laws must bear a significant causal relation to the party situation that will come to exist under them.

The best single case study in the causal relation between electoral system and party system is surely provided by a glance at the situation in Brazil. In Brazilian legislative elections, at both state and national levels, rules of perfect proportionality are observed; in addition, the voter votes not for the party as such, but for an individual candidate on the party's list. The result is not only a multiplication of parties (three major, two or three minor, and innumerable splinter parties exist) but a kind of war of all against all, since even candidates on the same party list are, to some extent, competing with each other for votes. This is the multi-party system carried to —and past—its logical conclusion. Yet in elections to fill single offices in Brazil, those of President, Vice-President, Governor, and Senator, the dynamics of the two-party system are clearly at work. Out of a welter of furious inter-group bargaining before each election emerge, in the typical case, two major coalition slates of candidates for the single offices to be filled; minor and splinter party third candidacies occur, especially as a consequence of stalemate and breakdown of the ticket-writing negotiations, but they are clearly hopeless gestures, about on the vote-drawing level of third-party candidacies in U. S. Presidential elections. This contrast between legislative and Presidential or Gubernatorial elections in Brazil provides a graphic illustration of the validity of the imputed causal relationship between the single-office election and the two-party system.[18]

The Multi-Party System. The multi-party system is the most widespread in Latin America, occurring in over half of the republics, although in different forms. The stability of the parties in such a system can vary over a wide range, from the situation in Chile, where the major parties, with one exception, are all over 50 years old, to that in Panama, El Salvador, or Haiti, where most parties do not date back more than two Presidential elections.

The relative importance in determining the voter's choice of the party itself, the party leader, and the individual candidate, also varies widely. As was noted, the influence of the personality of the party leader is greatest in the smaller and more backward republics. But the electoral laws are important here, too. It was mentioned previously, for example, that in Brazil the voter indicates his preference for the individual candidate, rather than for the party. Votes that the candidate receives over and above the quota necessary to elect him are credited to the other candidates on the party ticket. Particularly strong candidates are accordingly in a position to bargain with different parties for the best arrangement they can obtain, in terms of running-mates, the party's position on policy questions, etc.

---

[18] In Chile, victorious Presidential candidates normally represent coalitions also, but inter-party hostility is stronger than in Brazil, and coalition negotiations break down more frequently.

Under the Brazilian system, it was even possible for Jânio Quadros, a political independent, a man without party affiliation, to go all the way to the Presidency. In Chile, on the other hand, balloting arrangements make it easier for the voter to have a choice of voting either for an individual candidate or for the party list as a whole, which gives the party its own votes, as it were, making it less possible for an individual candidate to bargain with the party on terms of equality. Within the category of multi-party systems, then, there exists a wide latitude for variation in the degree of personalism, which will reflect provisions of the electoral laws as well as factors in the political culture of the country concerned. There is, however, a well-established syndrome of characteristics typical of the multi-party system as such.

In the first place, there is the tendency for the number of parties to proliferate indefinitely. If the nation's electoral laws allow small political groupings to secure legislative representation, there is obviously no inducement to channel political activity through an already existing party rather than create another one. To contain the party system within intelligible bounds, therefore, the standard practice is for the electoral laws to prescribe minimum conditions that parties must fulfill to be registered with the electoral tribunals and offer candidates. Apart from technical requirements, such as the reporting of the names of party officials, the key requirement is normally that a new party demonstrate a certain minimum of support before it can be registered; usually it must submit petitions containing a specified number of signatures. Although provisions of this type may act to exclude the most minuscule of splinter groups, a determined new party can usually find enough people to sign its petitions. Registration requirements, on the other hand, are liable to abuse, which occurs frequently, in being used by partisan officials to disqualify opposition parties and candidates on the basis of some minor technical infringement.

A more basic difficulty of the multi-party system is that, since the parties labor under no compulsion to try to put together a winning coalition of 50% + 1 of the voters for the legislative elections, they can afford the luxury of extreme and demagogic appeals that might alienate moderates but will win votes elsewhere. That is, in a multi-party system, it makes most sense for a party to fix on one or two substantial opinion-and-interest groups in the electorate, and try to capture their allegiance by outbidding the other parties for their support. The emphasis is not on moderation and inclusiveness, as in the classic model of the two-party system, but on extremism and one-sidedness, conducive to the deepening of political cleavages and a greater readiness to resort to violence.

This is a particularly explosive mixture in the multi-party system, because in the nature of things no one party will be able to gain a clear-cut electoral victory. The parties which, during the election, vied with each other in mutual vituperation, now find that the passage of legislation requires that they cooperate in forming a parliamentary majority. If such a majority can come into being— and it may not, creating a legislative stalemate and an invitation to Presidential dictatorship—it will be weak, internally divided, agreed only on a minimal program, and likely at any time to split and plunge the law-making processes into disorder. If the parties do manage to cooperate, on the other hand, even for a limited period, after an election campaign of mutual enmity and recrimination, this can only seem to the voter like the crudest kind of expediency which sacrifices principle to political ambition. The system has thus a built-in cynicism-producing effect.

Presidential elections in a multi-party system, subject to the dynamic processes of uninomial (single-office) elections, have the effect of inducing pre-election party coalitions, as was noted above. In Brazil and Chile, for example, attempts at forming coalitions for the Presidential elections are always made. In the two Presidential elections since the suicide of President Vargas (1954), the two parties founded by Vargas, the Social Democrats (PSD) and the Brazilian Labor Party (PTB), have run a coalition candidate against the anti-Vargas UDN (National Democratic Union). In Chilean Presidential elections since the 1930s, the parties of the Left have coalesced on a single candidate, a Radical where the Radical Party has joined the coalition, a Socialist where it has not; while the United Conservatives and the Liberals have likewise taken to running a joint candidate. In the 1958 Presidential election, these two coalition candidates were joined by one from the Christian Democratic party, which felt itself unable to join either coalition, and a representative of the Radicals, who could join with either but were undecided as to which.

Coalitions of a different type—"silent coalitions," one might say—have recently occurred in Presidential elections in Peru, Venezuela, and Argentina. During the periods of APRA's illegality in Peru, the party used unofficially to endorse the candidates of other parties; *Acción Democrática* acted similarly during the Pérez Jiménez dictatorship in Venezuela; while in the last Argentine Presidential election, exiled dictator Juan Perón urged supporters of his outlawed party to cast their votes for Arturo Frondizi, the candidate of the Intransigent Radicals.

Quite frequently, however, the successful Presidential candidate in multi-party elections represents a minority of the voters. The parties are too used to opposing each other in legislative elections to be able to coalesce on common Presidential candidacies. This necessarily means that the President will encounter great difficulties, in the legislature and in the country, in giving effect to his program.

Finally, the frequent mutations in the number of parties operating and in the coalitions formed, together with the ease with which a personalist leader can attract a following, mean that the system is in a constant state of flux, that quite different governing configurations emerge, and that policy lacks stability and continuity.

The Two-Party System. There are still what might be called two-party systems in several Latin American states: Colombia, Uruguay, Honduras, and Nicaragua, although in most of the republics the established two-party systems that were inherited from the nineteenth century were not able to contain the range of issues that became active during the twentieth century. The two-party system has preserved itself in each case for a variety of specific reasons, which may include: a favorable set of electoral laws (for example, the single-member district for legislative elections); the fact that the Liberal leaders proved flexible and open to new ideas; and a fierce inherited party loyalty stemming from memories of bitter civil war between the two parties.

Even where the two-party system continues in form, however, the range of political opinion has proved too broad to be expressed by only two alternatives, and the presence of more or less permanent factions within the two major parties is the standard situation. Permanent factionalism is especially characteristic of the two-party system, in point of fact; where party identification expresses an inherited loyalty, it is unavailable as an expression of opinion—to express a novel point of view, one creates a new faction rather than a new party.

Permanent factionalism is recognized by the Uruguayan electoral system, with provision being made for the combination of the votes cast for the factions within each party in the elections to the National Council, the country's collegial executive. In effect, the electoral law provides for a kind of simultaneous primary and general election, with victory going to the candidates of the majority faction of the majority party (who might have fewer votes than the candidates of the major faction of the minority party).

Permanently existing factions characterize the Colombian two-party system, also, the Conservatives being divided currently into Laureanistas and Ospinistas, after the names of the factional leaders, the Liberals being split between "doctrinaires," who form a substantial majority of the party, and the followers of Adolfo López Michelsen, who are organized as the Liberal Revolutionary Movement, or MRL.

In Nicaragua, also, the Liberal party has split as a result of its conversion into an organ of the dictatorship of the late Anastasio Somoza, currently being continued by his sons. The official party is the *Partido Liberal Nacional,* the anti-Somoza exile group taking the name *Partido Liberal Independiente.* The Conservatives have split along similar lines.

In Honduras the Nationalists (Conservatives) split between supporters and opponents of dictator Carías Andino; however, the two groups often cooperate and run joint candidates.

Thus, even in the normally two-party system, the groups actually competing for power may be more than one might guess on superficial acquaintance. On the other hand, a device has been developed for moderating the scope of the power struggle among the parties. This is guaranteed minority representation, which has replaced strict proportionality as the constitutive principle of some of the Latin American legislatures. Thus in Argentina, under the so-called Sáenz Peña law of 1912, which was revived after the overthrow of Perón but is scheduled to be replaced soon by a proportional representation system, minority parties are guaranteed at least one-third of the seats in the Chamber of Deputies by the provision that the voter can mark his ballot for candidates for only two-thirds of the vacancies. There used to be minority representation provisions in Cuban electoral legislation, also.

In Uruguay the principle of guaranteed minority representation is currently given effect in the republic's nine-man collegial executive, on which the seats are distributed in the ratio of six to three between the majority and the minority parties.

Colombia, as a result of the tragic experiences of over a decade of bitter guerrilla warfare between Conservative and Liberal partisans, together with the experience of cooperation between leaders of the two parties in the overthrow and liquidation of the dictatorship of General Rojas Pinilla, has gone a step further in this direction and established parity of representation for the two parties in all legislative organs and in the President's cabinet. This statesmanlike innovation, the National Front agreement, also stipulated that the two parties would alternate in the Presidency for a period of 12 years.[19] It was drawn up by party leaders Laureano Gómez for the Conservatives and Alberto Lleras Camargo for the Liberals in the Pact of Sitges of July, 1957, when both were in exile from the Rojas Pinilla dictatorship. Although the agreement was embodied in an amendment to the Constitution after the dictatorship was over-

[19] Subsequently extended to 16 years.

thrown, it is currently under attack from both ends of the political spectrum (having been repudiated by Laureano), although at present the weight of the country's opinion seems to continue in its favor, as was evidenced by the substantial margin of support given the National Front candidate in the 1962 Presidential elections.

The One-Party System. Perhaps most people would automatically identify a political system in which there was only one major party, in which everybody knew in advance that the government's Presidential candidate would be victorious, as a dictatorship. And certainly, most dictatorships do in fact establish an official party, which monopolizes electoral office, prohibiting or barely tolerating opposition groups. Present-day Cuba clearly falls into the category of the single-party dictatorship, for example.

On the other hand, there is in Mexico an example of a one-party system that tolerates the existence of opposition parties and candidates for office, and allows the full range of civil liberties one associates with a free and democratic state. Bolivia is a one-party state with a democratic system somewhat more limited than Mexico's. Today this does not seem quite as strange as it did a decade ago, since we have become familiar with the democratic one-party system in so many of the newly independent states of Africa and Asia (some of which have *non*-democratic one-party systems, also, to be sure).

At first sight, it certainly seems a paradox that a majority party which permits an opposition to develop can retain a monopoly on political power. Why are not all democracies two- or multi-party systems? Of course, in the long run, they are. Dissatisfaction with the incumbent party steadily increases until the opposition finds itself able to make a successful bid for power. But the long run can take a very long time to become reality. Thus, the conservative opposition party in Mexico, the Party of National Action (PAN), has steadily increased its vote in legislative elections since its founding over 20 years ago, but the rate of increase is slow enough that if it continues at the same amplitude, at the very least another 20 years will pass before the PAN can be within striking distance of a legislative majority. In other words, one-party politics represents a departure from an equilibrium two- or multi-party system, and some day the equilibrium position will be reached; but that day may be far off. Meanwhile, a democratic one-party system exists.

The PRI in Mexico and the MNR in Bolivia resemble African single parties in being based on a revolutionary nationalist *mystique,* and on the enthusiasm that nationalist revolution engenders. In neither does the importance of the charismatic leader approach the African norm, however. Moreover, each is based on a coalition of economic interest groups, with potentially conflicting interests, not on a population of fairly homogeneous economic character.

This necessity to reconcile the interests of a variety of economic groups has placed the leadership of the official parties of both countries under the necessity of performing miracles of conjuring and balancing in order to maintain the solidarity of the revolutionary party. This has been facilitated, and perhaps made possible, in Mexico by the existence of a steadily expanding economy, so that the claims of the various groups could be at least progressively satisfied without inhibiting the satisfaction of the claims of rival groups. The Bolivian leadership has been faced, to this point, with the all-but-impossible task of trying to pacify several key economic groups while the economy is actually shrinking; clearly, this kind of thing is possible only in the short run, and the success of the MNR in Bolivia is plainly contingent on the government's being able to reverse present economic trends.

Yet it is of first importance, in the years immediately following the Revolution, that these economic groups continue to maintain their uneasy alliance, for if they do not, armed conflict remains an ever-present possibility. Mexico has now passed that stage; Bolivia has not.

One could in fact regard the function of the one-party system as that of maintaining a balance among divergent interests long enough so that the habit of settling disputes by violence is lost. In this the Mexican party has in all probability succeeded, overcoming a historical tradition of constant civil war and political violence.

This is also the function that the Colombian National Front is designed to perform, using rather comparable techniques, although not the single-party mechanism.

The democratic one-party system can thus be viewed as a device appropriate to a stage of transition between the unity of a victorious revolutionary movement and the divisions of party politics normal to a democracy. Its value lies in allowing the turbulence of the revolutionary period to subside, in fostering patterns of peaceful politics, and by allowing the expression of views and the organization for political purposes normal to a democracy, while foreclosing the possibility that this will lead to violence and renewed civil war. However, it is solely valuable as making the transition possible, and if it succeeds it will eventually restore the country to multi-party politics. That is, in succeeding, the one-party system liquidates itself.

III   *Government Processes*

A. CONSTITUTIONS

THE GENERAL CONTENT OF CONSTITUTIONS

Constitutions always specify the organization of public powers; that is, they establish the various organs of government and define the relations among them. In addition, they set limits to the power wielded by the governmental structure as a whole—they define individual rights. Quite frequently, and especially today, constitutions indicate, often in considerable detail, the purposes government is designed to serve. In the recent constitutions, this latter function is carried to the point that the constitutional document contains what is in effect a general outline of the policies government should follow.

In their delineation of general governmental structure, the constitutions of the Latin American republics generally follow the constitution of the United States. Uniformly, they adopt the separation of powers, rather than the concentration of powers in the legislative body characteristic of parliamentary systems. With the exception of Uruguay, and presumably, today, of Brazil and Cuba,[1] they create strong Presidencies. Mexico, Argentina, Brazil, and Venezuela, in addition, have federal systems based on the North American model.

---

[1] At the time of writing, the Cuban constitution (of 1940) is in abeyance, and the Prime Minister, Fidel Castro, wields dictatorial powers, ostensibly in association with a "collective leadership" of members of his cabinet and others. The Brazilian constitution was amended in 1961 so as to reduce the powers of the President. The Uruguayan and Brazilian cases will be discussed later.

In the provisions governing individual rights, the courts, the administrative system, and the internal organization of the legislature, features of the Hispanic tradition are most in evidence, influenced by French innovations of the Revolutionary and Napoleonic periods.

In the sections on "social guarantees"—that is, those defining the general aims of policy with respect to labor, social welfare, and the economy in general—the strongest influence is probably that of the Mexican Constitution of 1917, the first of the "modern" constitutions in this respect.

THE FUNCTIONS OF THE LATIN AMERICAN CONSTITUTION

Quite clearly, many constitutional provisions are honored only in the breach; and yet great stress is placed upon constitutional forms and procedures, even where these mask political realities quite discordant with their intent. National constitutions are heavily eulogized in popular oratory, and key provisions are well known and frequently cited; yet existing constitutions are frequently discarded and replaced—in fact the average life of Latin American constitutions has been slightly less than 20 years.

Nevertheless, a common pattern does exist despite these paradoxes. One must distinguish, in the first place, between constitutional provisions that prescribe the distribution of public powers, which organize governmental authority, and those that enjoin or imply specific government policies. The latter clauses, those embodying "social guarantees," stipulating that education is free and compulsory, and so on, are not self-executing. They serve an exhortatory function, embodying national aspirations that should find expression in specific legislation and executive action where circumstances make this feasible. Provisions of this kind set a direction for public policy, prescribing ultimate goals rather than providing imperative mandates.

It is provisions of this kind that patriotic oratory regards as landmarks in the country's progress: the clause that establishes free public education as a national principle, or announces that subsoil minerals belong to the whole nation. In these provisions, the nation has taken a stand, adopted a certain orientation, and made its policy position clear.

The clauses that organize the public powers, prescribing the mechanisms of constitutional succession and establishing the organs of government, on the other hand, are literally followed in practice. It may well be that the constitutional forms do not correspond to political realities; the legislature is supposed to act independently of the President, although everyone knows it has no will of its own; the judiciary is supposed to be nonpolitical, although everyone understands that its decisions are guided by political *savoir-faire* rather than principles of jurisprudence. Nevertheless, the forms are observed, even where they seem to the onlooker merely ceremonial: the President proposes legislation, which the parliament goes through the motions of debating; the court hears evidence and hands down a learned decision that coincidentally favors the position adopted by the President.

Often the divergence between constitutional form and political reality is so great, however, that what occurs politically can simply not be contained within the terms of the fundamental law. When this happens, one does not simply violate the constitution; he rewrites it, to extend the dignity of constitutionality to the new situation. Normally, the dictator who wants to have a second term as President, when the constitution limits him to one, calls a constitutional convention to produce a new document; a successful revolution justifies itself retroactively by writing itself a new constitution; and so on. In any case, the successful revolution that is more than a simple palace revolt will want to provide itself with a new constitution to embody its principles in the nation's basic law. This signalizes the change in national orientation that has taken place, and is perfectly logical in the light of the meaning of revolution developed in the preceding pages.

An interesting variation on this theme occurs in Mexico, where not the constitution, but the organization and statutes of the ruling

Revolutionary party, have twice been reshaped with the accession to power of a new "strong President," representing a new political tendency. Since Calles founded the party as the PNR (National Revolutionary Party) in 1928, it has been reorganized twice, in 1938 by Lázaro Cárdenas as the PRM (Party of the Mexican Revolution) on the wave of nationalist feeling following the expropriation of the foreign oil companies, and by incoming President Miguel Alemán as the PRI (Party of Revolutionary Institutions) in 1946, symbolizing the party's coming to maturity and its swing to the Right.

AMENDMENT AND SUSPENSION OF CONSTITUTIONAL PROVISIONS

One might expect to find relatively easy processes of constitutional amendment, but this is not always the case. Amendment of the constitution, in every case, requires more than the simple plurality of the legislature necessary for the passage of ordinary law. At the least, passage of the amendment by the national Congress must occur on two occasions, separated by a decent enough interval that the public can be presumed to have had a chance to debate the amendment thoroughly. This is the rule in Peru and Ecuador. Congressional action on the amendment, too, always must be taken by an exceptional majority—not just a plurality of those voting, but a majority or even two-thirds of the total number of legislators. The requirement for a special convention to approve the amendment in addition to an affirmative vote of the Congress is common. Finally, the federal systems of Mexico and Venezuela assign the state legislatures, as well as the national Congress, a voice in the amendment process.

Even though the formal processes of amendment may seem to present obstacles to innovation, these obstacles, like those of the division of powers, can of course be overcome by a political movement that enjoys substantial support, and very little difficulty seems to have been experienced in fact in the amending of constitutions.

Amending the constitution, or more frequently, scrapping it and replacing it with his own, is a project high on the priority list of the dictator, regardless of how he comes to power. Even where he wins a free election and controls a majority of the legislature, provisions of a democratic constitution are likely to erect impediments to the smooth functioning of a dictatorship (although not as many as one might suppose, as will appear in the discussion of the Executive below). The first target for amendment is invariably the prohibition of the immediate re-election of the President, which is almost universal in Latin America.

Another aspect of the fact that constitutions are not the sacrosanct documents that one might expect is that typically the Latin American constitution itself permits the suspension of some of its provisions under emergency conditions. These are most commonly the provisions giving individuals immunity from arbitrary arrest and detention, and guaranteeing the political freedoms—speech, press, and assembly. These can be suspended—temporarily, although temporary emergencies have a way of dragging out—on the declaration of a state of siege, which is made by the President but normally, though not always, requires the concurrence of the legislative body; it is designed to be used in cases of foreign invasion, armed insurrection, and the like, but is generally used whenever opposition to the government seems likely to take a violent turn.

Uruguay is alone among the Latin American republics in having a constitution that makes no provision for a state of siege, although the Costa Rican constitution places heavy restrictions on the President's siege powers. While the stage of siege is supposed to be limited in time to the period of the emergency itself, it often happens that the declaration is renewed each time it expires, and any given President may govern during the greater part of his term under state-of-siege conditions. Thus, "constitutional dictatorship" becomes possible, and many good democrats—like President Betancourt of Venezuela—have found themselves forced by circumstances to suspend constitutional guarantees repeatedly. On the other hand, the state of siege device is more often used by authoritarian dictators to preserve a façade of legality for their regimes; using the state-of-siege provision, a President may be a notorious tyrant without violating the law in a technical sense.

B. THE LEGISLATURE

ORGANIZATION

In form, the Latin American legislature resembles the legislatures of continental Europe, modified by the addition of features similar to characteristics of the United States Congress.

The national legislatures each have two chambers, except for Paraguay and five out of the six Central American states.[2] The upper chamber (in every case, called the Senate) is always smaller than the lower (the Chamber of Deputies or Chamber of Representatives), and its members have longer terms of office. Accordingly, membership in the Senate is always more prestigious than belonging to the Chamber.[3] In Argentina, Brazil, and Chile, senatorial terms are staggered—that is, only part of the Senate is renewed at each election —as is the case in the United States. Elsewhere all Senators are elected simultaneously.

POLITICAL SIGNIFICANCE

Normally, the national Congress follows the President's lead, approving government bills and facilitating in other ways the government's performance of its functions. For most purposes, one can regard the policies followed by a Latin American country as the President's policies. There have been, however, numerous exceptions to this rule, and legislatures do pursue an independent line on occasion.[4]

Of the independent power of the Latin American legislature, one could say in general that it varies inversely with the political

[2] Guatemala, Honduras, El Salvador, Costa Rica, and Panama—all except Nicaragua, in other words.

[3] With the possible exception of Brazil.

[4] Of course in most countries of the world the government dominates the legislature, the United States Congress (especially the Senate) being one of the few surviving instances of a legislative body that actually writes the country's legislation itself. North Americans should accordingly be wary of treating their own national legislature as the normal case from which to measure deviations; it is actually highly exceptional.

strength of the President, and directly with the number of parties politically active. The first relationship is clear enough; the more the President controls the conduct of affairs, the less anyone else does, and *vice versa*. As to the second: the legislature can most assert its political independence of the President where a multi-party system exists, because in a two-party system, and certainly in a single-party system, the President's authority with the members of his own party will usually suffice to provide him with a majority in the legislative branch. Where the President's party is but one among several, however, he is more constrained to compromise with parliamentary leaders from groups other than his own to try to get their assent to his program, in which in any case he may fail. It is probably in Chile and Brazil, countries with continuing multi-party systems, that the President experiences the greatest difficulty in securing legislative support, although the national legislatures in Colombia and Venezuela frequently prove intractable; but legislative "rebellions" against the President's leadership have been known to occur in all the republics except those with overwhelming single-party control of the legislature.[5]

It is interesting to note that where the paths of President and legislature do diverge today, the legislature normally takes a position reflecting the special interests of individual groups in the society, the President's position being more in consonance with the interest of the nation as a whole. This difference in orientation between the two organs of state authority is becoming more notable today when the republics are being faced with the necessity of taking action to promote economic development which, while in the long-run interest of the nation, certainly damages the interests of specific economic groups in the short run. This problem will be taken up at greater length later, in the discussion of policy issues. At this point, however, we may note several interesting features of this emerging divergence in orientation.

One feature is that the defense of group interests by members of

[5] At the time of writing, Mexico, Bolivia, Paraguay, Nicaragua, and Haiti. The Cuban government currently functions without a formal legislature.

the legislature extends to the whole range of interests embraced by the country's economy. Most often it is still the interests of the wealthier sections of the community that find especial representation in the Congress. That is, "legislative rebellions" today take place typically over a land reform program that damages landowner interests or over the introduction, extension, or enforcement of an income tax law. This is to be expected in a class society in which the upper social groups are inevitably over-represented in the legislature (sometimes to the virtual exclusion of the lower) by virtue of their wealth, professional skills, and family connections.

However, it also happens that portions of a President's program that adversely affect the interests of wage-earners likewise engender legislative opposition, and reductions in the minimum wage or in the number of civil service employees are often as little likely to pass the Congress as the graduated income tax, in some cases even less so.

This situation is directly comparable to that in the United States, where the President has a national constituency and conceives of himself as acting in the interests of all the people, whereas the members of Congress are responsible primarily to districts in which specific interests predominate.

It is interesting to note that this situation differs from what the partisans of Presidency and legislature 100 years ago expected would evolve. In Latin America, as in the United States, the strong Presidency was regarded then as a bulwark of privilege and the *status quo,* whereas the popular house of the legislature was expected to represent the interests of the less affluent members of society. This expectation need not be exactly reversed today, but nearly so.

FUNCTIONS AND POWERS

The powers of the legislatures may be divided, for convenience, into three categories: legislative, censorial, and electoral.

The legislative functions are what one would expect; the parliament passes bills and resolutions. In addition, it approves or rejects proposed amendments to the constitution, although, as noted above, extraordinary majorities and in some cases special conventions are required. One should note that almost always the Congress acts on legislative drafts originating elsewhere, usually with the President and the cabinet; the Congress passes upon legislation, but does not initiate it.

The censorial functions of the parliament are those in the performance of which it acts as a watchdog or controller of the Executive. In the first place, the legislature may impeach the President and usually cabinet members and judicial officers. Where the legislature is bicameral, the standard arrangement is for the Chamber to impeach and the Senate to try, as in the United States. This power is rarely invoked, although it can be used by a dictator in the process of consolidating his power to remove the possibility of judicial opposition to his rule. Perón's controlled legislature, for example, removed the entire Argentine Supreme Court when it struck down government legislation as unconstitutional.

Normally, the Congress must approve the declaration of a state of siege, and sometimes has the power of disapproving actions taken by the President under his siege powers. It also often has the power to review and nullify decrees issued by the President.

In about half a dozen of the republics the legislature has the constitutional power of voting its lack of confidence in a member of the President's cabinet, who must then resign. This is a curious provision to find in a Presidential system, and can only be based on a misunderstanding of how such a system necessarily operates, since the President always sets the general direction of policy and *he* need not resign on a vote of "no confidence." To make one of his ministers resign, therefore, does not necessarily induce a change in the orientation of government policy; the President may simply find someone else to take over its implementation. To deny the legislature's confidence to one of the President's ministers can certainly be used in a guerrilla war against the President; but the ministers remain responsible to him, and not to the Congress.

Where provisions designed to enforce the responsibility of the cabinet to the Congress have been introduced, they have foundered on the Gibraltar of Presidential power, power not only legal in that it stems from provisions of the constitution, but also political in that a popularly elected President can count on public support far more than can the leaders of the legislature. Attempts to introduce cabinet responsibility in an otherwise Presidential system have uniformly led at best to failure, at worst to disaster. What they promote is, in effect, a running battle between the President and the Congress over control of the cabinet—for no strong President can simply surrender control of the cabinet to the legislature: he needs it to carry through his program and to perform successfully his role as head of the national administration.

This metaphoric war became a quite literal war in Chile, in 1891, when President Balmaceda tried to recover the authority over the cabinet that the constitution conferred on the President but that previous holders of the office had been content to relinquish to the national legislature. The war ended in a parliamentary victory and Balmaceda's suicide.

In 1947, in a similar showdown between President and Congress, Cuban President Grau San Martín broke an attempt to implement the parliamentary control of the cabinet that had been written into the constitution, by simply re-appointing to another cabinet post a minister who had resigned after losing a vote of confidence in the Congress.

In view of experience to date with the attempt to introduce parliamentary responsibility of the cabinet into the Presidential system, there seems no hope of success for the parliamentary system inaugurated in Brazil during 1961. At best by constitutional re-amendment, at worst by Presidential or military *coup d'état,* the system will be liquidated in the near future.[6] Responsibility of cabinet to legislature has so far succeeded in Latin America only in Uruguay, which has no President.

Similar observations might be made of Congress's power to confirm, or deny confirmation to, Presidential appointees to high posts

[6] Since this was written, the constitution has in fact been re-amended to eliminate cabinet responsibility, early in 1963.

and to the upper military ranks. It is a power over specific persons but not over the direction of policy.

Of particular interest among other miscellaneous censorial powers is the power of the Uruguayan and Chilean legislatures to appoint auditors, responsible to them, of the national accounts.

In line with the conception of Congress as censor of executive action is the tradition of a permanent commission, or committee, of Congress that functions during the period in which Congress is not in session, exercising Congress's powers of review of executive acts.

The electoral functions of the national Congresses are of two types: those which involve Congress's acting as a tribunal to pass on the validity of elections, and those in which Congress itself elects individuals to office. As an electoral tribunal, the Congress will perform various ceremonial operations in connection with the election of the President, but, more importantly, is the sole judge of the qualifications of its own members. That is, the outcome of a disputed election for legislative office can only be decided by the national legislature itself. Now clearly a Congress is not an impartial organ that will make determinations of this kind solely on the basis of the validity of the arguments on either side. It is unlikely, in other words, that the members of a party that has won a seat by fraud are going to vote against the party's retaining the seat, simply because of procedural irregularities alleged to be involved. It is much more likely that each legislator will vote in such a manner as to favor his own party, regardless of where the merits of the case lie.[7] This is especially so since in many disputed elections illegal activities can be shown to have been conducted on behalf of all the candidates. Thus, after each Congressional election in Mexico the public is regaled with endless tales of corrupt election practices and mutual recriminations among the parties, during the period in which the national legislature sits as an electoral tribunal. At the

[7] It seems to me that this occurs to a greater extent in Latin America, presumably because of the attitudes discussed in the previous chapters, than it does in the countries of Western Europe, where similar rules apply.

conclusion of the proceedings in the case of each disputed election, the legislative body votes on which candidate should be seated. But to verify the welter of charges that are made would occupy so much time, and would so frequently entail, in all likelihood, the disqualification of all the candidates, that in actuality the majority party, the PRI, votes in each case to confirm its own candidate (for whom inevitably the popular majority has been reported) in his seat, with the merest handful of seats being allowed the opposition parties. These are universally regarded as being in the nature of consolation prizes to the opposition, rather than as indicating that the candidate in question has actually the best title to be seated.

In addition to this indifferently performed role of electoral tribunal, the Congress itself acts for some purposes as an electoral college. In the dozen states without an elected Vice-President, Congress chooses the successor to a President who dies in office, retires, or who is unable to discharge his functions. This person (or persons) may be designated in advance, on the beginning of a new Presidential term; they will then be known, in the order in which they are to succeed, as First *Designado,* Second *Designado,* and so on. The title of *Designado* carries with it no duties, in contrast to the office of Vice-President, which normally entails presiding over the Senate. Alternatively, the President's successor may be designated only when the need has actually arisen. Then, often the person chosen will act as Provisional President only, until a new popular election can be organized. In the interim between the death or resignation of the President and the meeting of Congress called to pick his successor, the constitutional officer specified in the constitution itself—say, the President of the Supreme Court, often picked by the constitutional fathers as the least likely to try to perpetuate himself in office[8]—will serve as Provisional President.

If the constitution requires a stipulated percentage[9] of the popular vote for the election of a President (which no candidate may receive where several candidates are running) then the Congress is

[8] Too hopefully, experience has repeatedly shown.
[9] For example, in Honduras, 50 per cent; in Peru, 33.3 per cent.

empowered to choose a President from the leading candidates. In such a case, it is likely simply to pick the candidate who gained most popular votes—he will probably be uttering dire threats should the choice fall on one of his rivals, which may or may not have any effect. Of course it may happen that the legislators are unable to agree on a single choice; a legislative deadlock at such a time, however, is simply an invitation to a *coup d'état,* as Honduran experience has demonstrated.[10]

C. THE EXECUTIVE

THE POLITICAL SIGNIFICANCE OF THE LATIN AMERICAN PRESIDENT

In every country of Latin America except Uruguay and now Cuba, the President dominates the nation's government and politics. A glance at the political position of the President, and then at his legal powers, will show why this is necessarily the case.

Today, in all the republics having Presidential systems, the President is elected by popular vote. Electoral colleges in Peru, Argentina, Chile, and Cuba have been abolished within the last generation, and the power of electing the President taken from the hands of Congress in Haiti. This simple fact means that the President is necessarily one of the leading politicians in the country, usually the dominant political figure, and thus possessed of the personal popularity and authority that will cause his office to predominate over its rivals, irrespective of other factors. This is especially the case, as was noted previously, when the weakness of loyalties to institutional processes and political parties causes political life to center around personalities.

In addition, as one man, the President can easily be a more commanding figure than the Congress, where party in-fighting and the general stereotype of parliament as a place where only useless debating is done weaken the legislature in popular eyes. Moreover, the President is the undisputed head, as a general rule, of his political

[10] The latest instance of a *coup*'s taking place in Honduras when no candidate had a clear majority occurred in the fall of 1954.

party. This is likely to give him control of Congress; and frequently legislators are elected solely on the basis of their loyalty to the President or the Presidential candidate.

In his capacity as head of the Executive Branch, the President finds himself with many potent means of influencing opinion in his favor at hand. In a leading position is the patronage weapon, which plays a key role in Latin American politics. Furthermore, the discretion in the interpretation and application of the laws normally falling to the executive can be used to great effect to align political forces in the President's favor; export licenses and government bank loans can be withheld or granted; a projected road can pass this way or that; one scheduled irrigation project can be given priority over another; and so on.

Reinforcing, and being reinforced by, these political strengths of the President, there are also the considerable legal powers that normally attach to the office, which go much beyond those at the disposal of the United States President. The power to declare a state of siege has already been discussed; it enables the President, with the consent of the Congress if Congress is in session, to establish a temporary dictatorship and suspend individual freedoms, where the survival of the constitutional order is endangered. Of course this power lends itself to abuse, although conditions that do justify the imposition of a state of siege are in fact often present.

The power to issue decrees having the force of law also lies at the disposition of the President. Decree powers are known to all modern constitutions—even the United States has its executive orders, and Britain its Orders-in-Council—but their legitimate scope varies a great deal from one country to another. In the Latin American republics, the President's constitutional power of *reglamento,* the power to issue regulations necessary to supply gaps in Acts of the legislature, may be used to enact supplementary legislation. Presidential lawmaking on important questions occurs with much greater frequency, however, on the basis of delegations of power from the Congress authorizing the President to issue decrees on specific matters for specific periods, or under emergency decree-making powers that become available automatically on the declaration of a state of siege.

The President's powers over the spending of money are greater than those available in the United States (although in recent years the American Presidency has moved in the Latin American direction in some respects). Quite frequently the President, using his decree powers, can divert funds from one budgetary category to another, or even incur expenses over the budgetary allocation.

Finally, in the four federal states, the President has the power, in effect, of "firing" state governors and replacing them with his own appointees. In Venezuela, governors are in any case Presidential appointees. In Mexico, the federal Senate has the power of appointing a new governor where it finds that the constitutional authorities of the state have disappeared. No stringent definition of such a situation exists, and, normally, political criteria prevail, the Senate following the President's lead. In Argentina and Brazil the leading ground for the appointment of a federal "interventor" is in order to maintain a republican form of government (a phrase borrowed from the U. S. Constitution)—a very elastic contingency. Other grounds are provided, but are seldom needed. Presidents have used their decree powers to "intervene" other institutions, even private ones, such as labor unions or business firms, in similar fashion.

Perhaps one should add that, even with respect to the powers that the Latin American President shares with the United States President, he enjoys a more potent position. For example, his powers in relation to the legislative process are similar: he recommends laws, and can veto them. But in the majority of Latin American states, not only can the President propose laws, but the Congress will leave the drafting and introduction of legislation exclusively to the President. In almost every case, Congress has no legislative drafting office or legislative reference service that would enable it regularly to be the source of the legislative drafts on which it must pass, even if it were so disposed.

As can be seen from the preceding discussion, for most purposes one can consider a country's actions and policies as, in effect, those of the President. In fact, there occur cases in which, because of the amplitude of the legal powers of the President, and the preponderant role that even the most zealously constitutional President plays, it is an open question whether a given Chief Executive is a dictator or simply a strong constitutional President. We shall revert to this question when we come to consider Presidential dictatorship.

Because it is relatively easy, by overusing the powers legally available to him, for the President to tyrannize over the country, attempts have been made to limit the legal authority of the Presidency. We have already seen that the institution of cabinet responsibility to the legislature does not limit the President's pre-eminence, but instead impels him to abrogate the constitutional prerogatives of the parliament in order to play his accustomed role.

Occasionally, a President may allow a Prime Minister to be the actual director of policy, but no popularly-elected President need find himself under any compulsion to do so. One recent instance in which a Prime Minister was indeed allowed a wide range of authority was that of Pedro Beltrán of Peru, appointed to the office by President Manuel Prado, who (passing into his seventies halfway through his term) was no longer interested in maintaining a firm grip on the reins of policy in a situation in which economic circumstances called for drastic and unpopular measures to be taken.

Where a President does not in fact assume the vigorous leadership of affairs, this is likely to occur because of the weakness of a political position resulting from his election by a narrow segment of the electorate in a contest in which none of the several candidates became the overwhelming popular choice. In recent years, this was the case of President Ponce Enríquez of Ecuador, the narrowly elected candidate of a Conservative party[11] that was in a clear mi-

---

[11] Ponce Enríquez is actually leader of the small Christian Social Party, but was endorsed by the Conservatives and elected by Conservative votes.

nority position in the country. Such a President is able to count on support neither in the Congress nor among the people.

The most drastic way to limit the powers of the Presidency and insure against Presidential dictatorship is—to abolish the Presidency altogether! After pointing out that the two possible types of democratic government are the Presidential, involving a separation of powers (like that of the United States), and the parliamentary, involving the fusion of powers in the legislature (Great Britain), the textbooks have to add the afterthought, or footnote, that Switzerland has a political system that seems to fall properly in neither category: the collegial executive. In the Swiss system, which is rather like the commission form of municipal government, an executive council with members chosen for fixed terms collectively heads the Executive Branch (each member being responsible for a cabinet department) and collectively exercises the powers attributed to the Chief Executive in a Presidential system.

Under the influence of the great shaper of modern Uruguay, José Batlle y Ordóñez, the Uruguayans have experimented with a collegial executive similar to the Swiss. The form of *colegiado* now in operation, which was installed in 1952, differs from the Swiss in several respects, however. In the first place, members of the National Council do not themselves head executive departments but rather supervise a cabinet whose individual members are responsible to the legislature. This dual responsibility of the cabinet may not necessarily have the disastrous consequences that have attended it in Presidential systems, however, because the collegiality of the executive dilutes its power to defy the legislature, and makes an attenuated parliamentary government possible despite the separation of powers.

The National Council is itself elected by popular vote (for a four-year term), with the majority party assigned six, and the minority three, Council seats. Clearly, the plural executive cannot act as decisively, nor build up as much popular support behind a new program, as can a single President. While this weakness will not prove to be, in the peaceful, firmly democratic, Uruguayan welfare state, the danger it would in a turbulent state with an accumulated back-log of urgent problems, it remains to be seen whether even Uruguay can afford the slow pace and indecisiveness of a collegial executive.

One method that all the republics, with the sole exception, today, of the dictatorships of Haiti, Cuba, and Paraguay, have adopted to limit the evolution of the constitutional President into a dictator, is to stipulate that no President can succeed himself in office. In most of the republics an ex-President may be re-elected to the office after "skipping" a term, however, and it is common for ex-Presidents to make comebacks. In the last decade ex-Presidents Vargas (Brazil), Ibáñez del Campo (Chile), Velasco Ibarra (Ecuador), Betancourt (Venezuela), Prado (Peru), Paz Estenssorro (Bolivia), and Lleras Camargo (Colombia) have all returned to the Presidency after a lapse of time. For example, two of the candidates in the Costa Rican Presidential elections of 1962 were ex-Presidents (neither of them emerging the victor on that occasion).

PRESIDENTIAL DICTATORSHIP

Usurpation of the President's Office. Given the prohibition of im-mediate re-election as a guarantee against the erection of a dictator-ship, it follows that the President who would make himself a dictator—with occasional curious exceptions—must somehow cir-cumvent this provision. In abrogating the prohibition of re-election, or in offering himself for re-election, a President thus crosses the Rubicon and takes leave of generally accepted constitutional norms, no matter how careful he has been up to that point to secure a legal façade for his actions by procuring Congressional grants of delegated legislative powers, and the like.

The sharp break with the constitutional tradition entailed in the violation of the prohibition of re-election is the kind of act that would-be dictators try to avoid, as it only serves to strengthen and consolidate the opposition and alienate the uncommitted. To the maximum extent possible, the dictator tries to contain his acts within the bounds of legality—for the sake of administrative coherence and the obtaining of a good press abroad, as well as to avoid unnecessary domestic opposition. A great deal of rewriting and amending of constitutions is invested in this effort, of course. Consider the case of Getúlio Vargas: coming to power at the head of a revolt in 1930, he ruled as "Provisional President" until 1934; in that year a constitutional convention rewrote the nation's fundamental law, terminating its work by electing Vargas the first "Constitutional President" to serve under its provisions; toward the end of his term, in 1937, Vargas staged a *coup d'état,* abrogated the 1934 constitution, and decreed a new one, which remained legally in effect, though honored more in the breach than the observance, until he was forced to resign the Presidency in 1945.

In point of fact, the expiration of his term of office is always a time of crisis for the dictator-President. Normally, he attempts to continue in the office himself; sometimes, he merely tries to impose his own choice as successor; occasionally, a dictator will preside over relatively free elections to choose the man to succeed him—Batista did this in 1944, for example, Odría in 1956. In the first two types of situation, revolts are frequent, made before the election by the opposition or by a member of the ruling group passed over for the regime's nomination, or after the election by a defeated candidate charging fraud, or by a populace disgusted with the travesty on democratic procedures they have witnessed. In Mexico of the 1920s, for example, revolts accompanied, immediately preceded, or immediately followed the Presidential elections of 1920, 1924, 1928, and 1929 (the last for Provisional President, following the assassination of the President-elect). Similarly, United States intervention in Cuba under the terms of the Platt Amendment, to ensure the continuation of constitutional processes, occurred during the revolts and attendant civil wars that followed the Presidential elections of 1906, 1912, and 1916.

The wise dictator, cognizant of the problem of the re-election crisis, finds ways of short-circuiting the crisis period, or tries to. Probably the most successful method is the one used by Vargas in 1934—to call a constituent convention that itself elects the dictator to the first term under the provisions of the new document that it drafts. This circumvents the popular agitation to which an election campaign gives rise, and indeed does not even allow the crystallization of opinion around rival candidates. Maximilian Hernández Martínez of El Salvador executed this maneuver twice, having constituent assemblies elect him to a new term in 1939 and again in 1944.

An original device to secure his continuance in office was contrived in 1961 by President Duvalier of Haiti. Duvalier had his name printed at the head of the ballot for members of Congress for the legislative elections occurring halfway through the six-year Presidential term, and then announced that he had been re-elected President for a new term without opposition.

The danger that an election too obviously and heavy-handedly rigged can create for the dictator is illustrated by the fate of Pérez Jiménez in Venezuela. The dictator's henchmen organized a plebiscite in place of the election scheduled for 1957, with voters able to deposit a "Yes" or "No" card indicating whether or not they favored the continuance of Pérez Jiménez in office. Various techniques were adopted to ensure that the outcome would be favorable to the regime —for example, government employees (who form a substantial proportion of the population) were required to report for work on the day following the election with their "No" cards, as evidence that they had not been cast, resident foreigners were allowed to vote,[12] and so on. General popular disgust with the whole farce contributed directly to the military *coup* that unseated Pérez Jiménez shortly after the "plebiscite." The dictator might have had better luck if he had relied on the maneuver used at the election of the constitutional assembly that first named him to the Presidency five years before. Then the military *junta* ruling the nation had simply announced a set of election results in conformity with its wishes, although not with the votes cast, after preliminary returns had suggested that the election was going "the wrong way."

[12] Venezuela has large numbers of residents of Spanish and Italian origin especially. Under United States law U. S. citizens may forfeit their citizenship for voting in a foreign election, however.

There are three types of methods an incumbent administration can use to "rig" elections so as to continue itself in office. The first, which consists simply of falsifying the returns, already has been cited. By this technique it is possible to achieve a favorable outcome even where opposition parties may campaign freely and voters may cast their ballots as they choose. Difficulties for this approach may be presented, however, by demands of the opposition parties to be represented on election tribunals and in the process of tallying the vote. Nevertheless, what might be called arithmetical fraud is quite widespread in Latin America (it is not unknown elsewhere!), and even where the national government itself attempts to conduct an honest election it occurs at the local level.

An incumbent government can also influence the outcome of an election in which the votes are fairly counted, by throwing the weight of its official powers behind the regime's own candidate. Perhaps this technique reached its maximum effectiveness under Perón, whose election victories were apparently genuine ones in an arithmetical sense. Perón's government would allow opposition candidates, but would subject them to extreme harassment and make it impossible for them to campaign. Opposition newspapers were closed under various pretexts, the use of the radio was denied opponents of the regime, and so on.

Finally, often elections are held with only a single candidate competing. The attractiveness of democratic ideals, however much belied by dictatorial realities, remains so great that authoritarian governments feel that even this type of "election" confers a measure of legitimacy. The regime may have outlawed all candidacies save the official one, or opposition parties may have boycotted the election because they knew the vote would not be counted fairly in any case (although sometimes opposition parties stage a boycott and make this charge simply to save face when they know they would stand no chance in a fairly tallied vote).

By one means or another, *imposición,* the imposition on the voters of an "official" candidate, regardless of their preferences, is a general practice. In the entire history of several of the republics no Presidential candidate sponsored by the incumbent administration has ever been defeated in a popular election. This has on occasion been because he was in reality the popular choice, of course.

Because of the prevalence of *imposición,* it is not enough to assume that a President who traces his title to a popular election is a legitimate democrat, whereas one who came to power through a revolt is a dictatorial usurper. The popular election in question may have been thoroughly rigged, whereas the revolt may have been a genuine expression of the popular will, forced to take the path of revolt because it had been frustrated by the corruption of the electoral process. Woodrow Wilson's policies with respect to Latin America frequently came to grief because of his failure to understand this point.

Dictatorial Government. The medievals, who had much experience with tyrants, and, especially because of religious scruples, wished to be clear at what point they were justified in withholding their allegiance from a ruler or conspiring to overthrow him, used to distinguish between the tyrant by usurpation, the ruler who had no legitimate claim to his position, and the tyrant by performance, who may have had a legitimate claim, but forfeited it by his conduct in office.

This distinction can be suggestive for our present purposes. The tyrant by usurpation, the President who owes his sash of office to a *coup d'état* or a falsified election, has certainly no legitimate title, and thus provides a sufficient ground for honorable men to oppose him. It is possible, on the other hand, for a President to command popular support and to win election after election and be a tyrant nevertheless. This is a point that was often lost sight of in the disputes over the ambiguous character of the government of Fidel Castro that took place during 1961, with one side arguing that, as he refused to hold elections, he was a dictator, the other that elections were divisive and wasteful, and in any case unnecessary since Fidel obviously had majority support. There are things beside elections that determine whether or not a man is a dictator, after all.

Until now, the discussion has been premised simply on the postulation of a dichotomy between democracies and dictatorships. Actually, considerable variations are possible within the category "dictatorship." When we discussed the role of the army in politics, for example, we distinguished between the dictatorship which was of the army, by the army, and for the army, as it were, and the *personal* dictatorship of a leader who happened to be a professional soldier.

One of the simplest, and yet one of the most helpful, ways of distinguishing among dictatorships is to consider how dictatorial they actually are—that is, to introduce the notion of different degrees of dictatorship. This is clearly a factor of central importance to the person who lives under the dictator, and may justifiably influence one's moral evaluation of the system. Although both were surely dictators, for example, there was a world of difference between the rule of Getúlio Vargas, which was on the whole a mild and easygoing authoritarianism, and the institutionalized reign of terror of a gangster such as Trujillo. It is interesting to note that the dictators themselves are rather sensitive about differences of this kind. It was reported of the late Anastasio Somoza of Nicaragua—not himself a particularly benevolent ruler—that he resented the tactics used by Trujillo as tending to give "strong Executive rule" a bad name, and he used to object strenuously to being classified with the Dominican tyrant. General Stroessner of Paraguay, similarly, takes pains to point out the differences between himself and Trujillo, laying stress on his claim that he "never had a man killed" except for armed rebels who died fighting against his government.

Completely totalitarian government, absolute dictatorship over every political and social institution—government, army, university, Church—and over every act and utterance of every citizen, is not achieved immediately, of course. The dictator who would be totalitarian engages in a continuing series of political battles with every source of potential opposition until he can feel sure that he rules alone and unchallenged. Of course, he can never be perfectly sure, and the secret political police must be continually busy. The career of Perón is instructive in this regard: in successive skirmishes the unions, the army, the judiciary, and the universities were "co-ordinated" with the regime; Perón fell in the struggle to establish his mastery over the navy and over the Church.

As C. W. Cassinelli has pointed out, totalitarian rule is necessarily personal rule. The totalitarian dictator maximizes his power by sharing it with no one; he balances his party off against the army, against the Church perhaps, against the unions, against the officials of government; perhaps only his secret police wields independent power, and it is itself kept in a continual state of turmoil. The stage of secret police domination of the state is thus also the period of maximum deification of the ruler; personalism and terror join hands. This was clearly the case in the heyday of Stalin's rule, and so it was under Trujillo; so it is becoming under Duvalier. The statues of the Leader are erected to the accompaniment of gunfire in the back alleys and screams from the torture chambers.

Few Latin American dictatorships actually become totalitarian—in recent years probably only those of Trujillo and Castro could be enumerated, with Perón failing in the attempt. For the most part, the Latin American dictator rests content with something less than totalitarian power. It normally suffices him if his orders are carried out and his government unopposed; in many cases the opposition is permitted a moderate amount of activity, so long as this does not actually threaten the dictator's grip on the apparatus of government. Under Vargas, for example, the courts occasionally held his acts unconstitutional and still continued to function unmolested—although he continued with his "unconstitutional" policies as though nothing had happened! Minimal dictatorship of this kind is most likely, however, where the dictator is concerned solely with either feathering his nest to the maximum in the shortest possible time (for example, the first years of Batista's rule after his comeback in 1952) and/or with preserving the *status quo* on behalf of the old ruling classes. The strong ruler interested in putting through a program will ordinarily not be as forbearing with the opposition as Vargas was.

The single most important fact one should note about the cabinet in any Latin American country is that, as under any strong-President constitution, it can, politically speaking, only be an appendage to the Chief Executive. The President necessarily determines the direction of policy; the cabinet is simply a collection of the President's chief administrative and technical assistants. This is true regardless of what the constitution may say about the parliament's powers with relation to the appointment and dismissal of ministers.

There are occasional exceptions to this general rule, where a President is enfeebled by age or sickness, or is simply not an assertive person, and a leading member of the cabinet comes to dominate the administration. They are rare, however, and limited to individual cases, for the reason that feeble, shy, or unassertive men are hardly likely to be elected to high office in the first place.

Usually there are about 12 members of the President's cabinet, with the size of the individual bodies currently ranging from 9 to 24 members. As in the United States, separate agencies and commissions are often established, some continuing on a permanent basis, with heads who report directly to the President.

Within the cabinet itself, the relative importance and political weight attached to the holders of the various portfolios varies. It is suggestive to regard some cabinet positions as being more "political," others as more "technical," although of course all are both to some degree. The most "political" members of the cabinet will normally be the Secretary of *Gobernación* or Interior, the Secretary of War or Defense, the Secretary of the Presidency, where one exists, plus in Mexico and Venezuela the Governor of the Federal District, and in Honduras the mayor of the capital city, Tegucigalpa, who are also members of the cabinet. These individuals will usually be the most important in domestic politics, the most influential, and the most likely prospects for future Presidential candidates.

A special word is in order about the Secretary of *Gobernación,* who has no exact equivalent in the United States, although his func-

tions resemble those of Ministers of Interior in most countries.[13] His
responsibilities fall into several categories, encompassing principally
the supervision of provincial and local government, the administration of elections, and the control of the national police. One can see
the reason for his title, Minister of Government—although it might
as well be Minister of Politics since, in an administration so disposed, he is in a position to manipulate election results, create a
patronage system in local government tied to the ruling party, and
use force against opposition elements. In any case, his job requires
a great deal of political skill and general *savoir-faire,* and makes him
often the second man in the government, after the President. In
several of the republics, in addition, the Interior and Justice portfolios are regularly held by a single member of the cabinet.

If the Secretary of *Gobernación* is not the second most important
official of the administration, chances are that that distinction falls
to the Minister of Defense (or whatever designation is given the
minister who has political responsibility for the army). In 13 of the
republics, this is a single Minister of Defense or of the Armed
Forces, whereas 3 countries have separate ministers for each service.[14] Argentina has a combined system, not unlike that of the
United States, except that the Minister of Defense *and* the Secre-
taries of State of each armed service all have seats in the cabinet.
Costa Rica and Panama, which have no armed forces as such, have
no cabinet portfolios for military departments; supervision of the
national police in each country comes under the jurisdiction of the
Minister of *Gobernación*.

The political weight of the Minister of Defense varies, of course,
with the importance of the army in the country's politics. But even
in the more politically developed states, it is still customary for the
minister responsible for the armed forces to be himself a ranking
military officer, who is regarded more or less as the representative
of service interests.

The Minister for Foreign Affairs is invariably the ranking "tech-

[13] In Great Britain, the Home Secretary.
[14] Mexico, with two armed services, and Brazil and Peru, with three.

nical" minister, and is quite often a distinguished figure in the life of his country, a respected scholar, jurist, or man of letters. He is rarely a key party politician, however, and in many countries his job has almost a non-partisan aura about it. Foreign Ministers become Presidential candidates much less frequently than one might assume from the intrinsic importance of the position, partly because of this factor, partly also because the Minister has usually spent a good deal of time out of the country in lesser diplomatic posts and has not built up a political following; and often because, either as Foreign Minister or in a previous tour of duty as Ambassador to the United States, he came to be regarded as too pro-Yankee.

The portfolios of Education and, sometimes, Justice are generally occupied by similar types, the distinguished professor or jurist who is not really a party politician. Frequently, when a vacancy occurs to head the Foreign Office it is the Minister of Education who is promoted.

THE PUBLIC SERVICE

In the modern state, the public service, ideally, is supposed to be politically neutral, to confine itself to technical administrative tasks within the policy guidelines established by the country's elected political leadership. To insulate civil servants from political interference, and to eliminate partisanship in the staffing of non-political positions, holders of bureaucratic office are given security of tenure, being liable to dismissal only for grave faults, and then only after a rigorous procedure has been followed. This security of tenure acts, in addition, to attract candidates of ability to the public service; recruitment—again, ideally—depends solely on merit, as tested by competitive entrance examination.

Clearly, the merit system can work as it should only under certain special social and political conditions. Security of tenure can best be assured in a polity that is stable and commands general popular support; where the accession of a new leadership to power does not imply a change of policy so great that holders of administrative office under the previous regime must be assumed to be disloyal to the new one. To go a step further, one might say that the merit system works best in a classless society, where general equality of opportunity in education means that civil service examinations discriminate only on the basis of ability and not on social class.

Viewed in this perspective, it is clear that for the most part the states of Latin America are not well equipped to have modern bureaucracies working for them. They are a long way from equality of opportunity in education; frequent turmoil provides an unfavorable setting for security in tenure; low standards of political morality undermine principles of merit recruitment and tenure—in cases known to the writer, offices have actually been sold: one received an appointment on payment of a fee. Moreover, the tradition of personalism makes it likely that loyalties will be to individual political leaders, not to abstract institutions.

It is possible to argue that, in their present stage of development, a merit bureaucracy would not be functional in view of the needs of most of the Latin American states. From the point of view of the leader who has just come to power, for example, merit or seniority may be of secondary importance to loyalty as a consideration in making key appointments. This is certainly the case if the country has a tradition of violent change of government. Often a President who left in office the functionaries of his predecessor's regime had cause to regret it—Francisco I. Madero, for example, who was deposed and shot by a military commander he should have replaced when he came to power.

One might argue, further, that a spoils system of appointments might have advantages if it were used to create enduring parties in those countries where at present parties are fluctuating personalist groupings. A very good case against a merit bureaucracy could be made, too, in the light of the colossal problems that face Latin American governments: security of tenure makes for complacency, devotion to routine, unimaginativeness, lack of initiative, whereas the obstacles to social development in the Latin American states can be surmounted, if at all, only by individuals chosen for their devotion to the programs and goals of the government leaders.

Despite the difficulties and the negative arguments, however, attempts have been made to introduce elements of a modern system of public administration to some of the countries of the area. Today, at least some features of the merit system can be found in nearly all the republics. Some states—most notably Brazil and Costa Rica—have established central personnel agencies, which set common general policies; but the general rule is that recruiting and promotion policies are set by each agency for its own personnel, and not on a government-wide basis. This makes a certain amount of sense, but results in inequalities and budgetary difficulties of all sorts, in addition to making bribery and kick-backs harder to eliminate. As a result, the merit system comes soonest to those agencies—for example, the public health services—which perform the most technical tasks, for which qualifications over and above the ties of personal friendship and family relationship are clearly required.

A crucial problem is that one of the features of the merit system —security of tenure—is readily adopted without the simultaneous adoption of the provisions that complement it, or in polities whose other characteristics lend no support to the development of a modern bureaucracy. Regulations protecting tenure are easy to adopt because they are favored by the civil servants themselves, and also by the incumbent administration, which wants to blanket its followers into tenure positions before it leaves office. As a result, a new administration finds that it cannot get rid of the public servants it has inherited. Rather than assuming the unlikely: that they are impartial and non-political and can be expected to perform loyally, the new government simply creates a set of new positions, which it then fills with the deserving among its own supporters. Thus, the public service swells, the necessary work is spread thinner, and red tape starts to multiply. But this process occurs again with the advent of each succeeding new government. The end result is that civil service jobs become part-time or sinecure positions, which are regarded as such, and are compensated accordingly. This in turn provides a further reason for expecting a *mordida,* or petty bribe, from the hapless citizen, who must pay it or expect his claim, or request, to be lost from sight forever in the mass of paperwork that clogs the channels of administration. Perhaps the leading victim in Latin America of this ailment—the swollen bureaucracy—is Venezuela, with Brazil following closely.

It is unlikely that a government can attempt drastic measures to break out of the vicious circle of the over-expanded part-time bureaucracy, despite its inefficiency and expensiveness. To do so would be to throw many out of work in a society where unemployment is already too great, to make enemies of educated people living in the capital city, which is hard enough to control at the best of times, only, in many cases, to replace the expense of their salaries by expense almost as great for pensions and unemployment benefits and other forms of government compensation.

D. THE JUDICIARY

The legal systems of Latin America are comparable to those of the continental European countries, rather than of the countries where English is spoken, in their form, origins, content, and political implications.

THE CHARACTER OF THE LAW

The origins of the basic concepts of the legal systems of the area are traceable, ultimately, to Roman law, mediated through colonial law, and through the Napoleonic Code and the Spanish codes based on it, which have been extensively copied in Latin America. These concepts often result in rules on matters of substance at variance with the rules one finds in systems based on the English common law—on such points as inheritance and the character of property rights, for instance. Of more importance from the point of view of politics, however, may be the general difference in the structure of the two types of law. The one is "code" law, with the provisions applicable to principal fields systematized into codes, whereas the English system is based on "common" law, essentially the whole array of precedents that represent the decisions of judges in specific cases dating back over 1,000 years. Many observers have contended that the differences between the two types of legal system result in differences of habits of mind among lawyers that in turn affect the style of political life. Under a common law system, it has been argued, students are trained to regard the law as flexible, and matter for argument; they are taught by the case method, which induces pragmatism and inductive modes of thought; while the courts use the adversary method of pleading cases (Smith *versus* Doe), which promotes open-mindedness and an acceptance of the legitimacy of differing points of view. Under the "code" system (the argument goes on), the existence of the sum total of valid law in codified form promotes a closed-minded and dogmatic approach; legal instruction stresses deductive reasoning and a reliance on authority not conductive to democratic attitudes; this is fortified in turn by the more restricted role allowed counsel, and the greater latitude given the judge, in proceedings under the codes. Although influences of this subtle a character are hard to trace specifically, it seems reasonable that they have been active at least to some extent in helping to shape the political culture of the Latin states.

One should note that there have been United States influences in some areas of Latin American law—especially on constitutional law, since institutions modeled on those of the United States have found their way into the political system. In the federal systems, for example, precedents of U. S. courts are cited in support of judicial decisions on federal questions. It is doubtful, however, that many borrowings from the common-law countries can be successfully absorbed into systems of law of such basically different character. The jury system, for example, has been tried intermittently, but in general found to work badly; juries are reluctant to convict, for one thing, perhaps because of a different traditional attitude toward authority.

THE POLITICAL STANDING OF THE JUDICIARY

Invariably, the constitution establishes the judiciary as an independent organ, standing on an equal footing with executive and legislature. The political reality is at variance with the constitutional norm, however, and the courts have a relatively limited sphere of political action in relation to the executive, although in most cases they play a more independent role than does the legislature.

The degree of independence the judges have depends, in the first instance, on their freedom from influence by the executive. This depends in turn primarily on their security in office; where judicial appointments are made for life (or "during good behavior," which is normally equivalent to a life appointment), judicial decisions are freer than if the judge has to consider what the effect of his decision will be on his chances for reappointment or for re-election by the legislature. Judges of the highest court serve indefinite terms in Argentina, Brazil, Chile, Peru, and now in Mexico. Formerly, indefinite terms were the rule in Cuba, too. In addition, judges in Uruguay, Colombia, and Costa Rica can regularly expect to be confirmed in office when their terms expire. Elsewhere, there is great pressure on judges not to hand down decisions that will be unpopular with President and Congress.

It is also true that the degree of discretion available to a judge is less under a code-law system, where, in principle, the code specifies the decision that is to be reached under every possible set of circumstances, than it is under the common law, where a variety of precedents may exist that allow a judge greater discretion in arriving at his decision. There is nevertheless some latitude within which a range of interpretations of the law is possible even under the most detailed code. Perhaps the sharpest limitation on the role the courts can play in politics in the Latin American republics, as contrasted with the United States, is that under the typical Latin American constitution itself the President is given so much power that the Supreme Court, interpreting the constitution, can erect few impediments to his actions.

The courts' powers to decide questions of constitutionality are limited in another way. A court may find that the application of the law in question to the case in hand would violate the constitution; but this finding is limited in its effect to the specific case being tried—it does not nullify the law. In some countries, an uninterrupted series of decisions to the same effect will create binding precedent, however: five decisions in Mexico, and three in Colombia, in some types of case.

A final limit on the political significance of the courts is that controversies in several fields, often those most germane to political issues, do not come before the regular court system, but before special judicial bodies or tribunals. This is generally true in Latin America with respect to issues relative to elections, for example, to labor questions, to questions of administrative jurisdiction, and to tax questions. For litigation in each of these areas, a separate set of tribunals frequently exists, operating under different ground rules and usually more subject to political influence than the regular court system.

Still, the courts do play a certain political role on occasion, especially in the defense of individual rights. Lacking the means of enforcing their decisions, however, they cannot be expected to provide any substantial defense against the imposition of tyranny; the fact that the milder dictators permit the courts to continue to function normally (Getúlio Vargas, for example) should be regarded not as evidence of the strength of the courts, as it has been by some commentators, but as an indication of their ultimate political weakness.

E. NATIONAL-LOCAL RELATIONS

Due to the vastness of the territory that most of the Latin American republics encompass, and the natural barriers to communication that exist, local officials inevitably exercise a great deal of discretion, regardless of the legal and constitutional framework within which they function. In addition, there is a sort of *mystique* of the "free" municipality, with its *cabildo* or council regulating local affairs, which continues to be influential. There has indeed always been a Hispanic tradition of municipal autonomy, although this has been steadily reduced in Spanish America, in part by the improvement in communications, with the early days after Independence probably representing the high point that municipal autonomy has reached.

Four of the Latin American states are federal republics: Mexico,

TABLE II *Major Political Features of the Latin American States*

	Normal Political Role of Military	Party System	Presidential Term	Other Features
Costa Rica	None	Multi-party	4 years	Unicameral legislature; many agencies independent of Presidential control
Bolivia	Limited; also Party militia	M.N.R. dominant	4 years	
Chile	Limited	Multi-party	6 years	Tradition of strong legislature
Colombia	Limited	Conservatives and Liberals (both in factions)	4 years	National Front till 1976: parties share all posts, alternate in Presidency
Mexico	Limited	P.R.I. dominant	6 years	Weakly federal
Uruguay	Limited	Colorado and Blanco (both in factions)	National Council (4 years)	Parties seated 6-3 on Council; cabinet responsible to legislature
Brazil	Intervene	Multi-party	5 years	Cabinet responsibility to legislature; federal
Ecuador	Intervene	Fluctuating multi-party	4 years	Some Senators represent functional groups
Honduras	Intervene; also National Guard	Liberal and 2 Nationalist parties	6 years	Unicameral legislature

Panama	National Police; intervene	Unstable, personalist	4 years	Unicameral legislature
Peru	Intervene	Multi-party	6 years	Cabinet nominally responsible to legislature
Argentina	Veto power	Multi-party	6 years	Parties share Chamber seats 2/3-1/3 by province; weakly federal
Dominican Republic	Veto power	Emergent multi-party (?)	4 years; re-eligible	In transition from dictatorship
Guatemala	Veto power	Multi-party	6 years	Unicameral legislature
Haiti	Veto power	Nebulous	6 years; re-eligible	Currently personal dictatorship
Venezuela	Veto power	Multi-party	5 years	Nominally federal
Cuba	Revolutionary army; in control	O.R.I. dominant	Constitution of 1940 in suspension; Prime Minister dictator though associated with "collective leadership"	
El Salvador	In control	Fluctuating	6 years	Unicameral legislature
Nicaragua	In control	2 Conservative, 2 Liberal parties	6 years	Somoza family dictatorship
Paraguay	In control	Colorados dominant	5 years; re-eligible	Unicameral legislature; permanent dictatorship

Argentina, Brazil, and Venezuela. The others are unitary states. The formal difference is this: in a federal system, the member-states of the federation have reserved powers that the federal government may not assume, and they may act in areas of policy that are forbidden to the federal government. To guarantee their retention of their rights under the system, the states must participate in the process of constitutional amendment, certainly if the alteration of their own status is contemplated. In the unitary scheme, on the other hand, there may be considerable provincial autonomy, but legally this is only permitted by the central government at its pleasure, and does not exist for the provincial government as a right.

One would expect to see a great difference between the unitary and the federal systems, then, in the powers concentrated at the level intermediate between national and local government, that of the state, province, or department, corresponding to the different constitutional-legal principles involved. In actuality, the differences are not great. The governors of the states of the Venezuelan federation are even appointed by the national President, for example, whereas on the other hand many constitutions organized along unitary lines provide for elected provincial assemblies, and two—those of Cuba and Uruguay—envisage an elected provincial executive. In any case, the practice of federal intervention, and the holding of a federal power to intervene in reserve, means in effect that the states of Mexico or the provinces of Argentina are not much different in powers from the departments of Chile, say. Emilio Portes Gil, the former President of Mexico, has frankly called Mexican federalism "a great lie." Only in Brazil (except for its period under the dictatorship of Getúlio Vargas) can one consistently see states genuinely pursuing courses of action independent of the federal government, and even conflicting with it, with impunity, comparable to what takes place in the North American states or the Canadian provinces. Brazil has a relatively strong tradition of state autonomy, understandable given the colossal size of the country, which flourished especially in the 40 years between the abdication of the Emperor and the accession to power of Getúlio Vargas. Vargas replaced the elected state governors by his appointees, and ended the independence of the states, but it has since revived and today stands clearly in a different category from the position of the states in Mexico or Argentina.

Federal intervention, which was referred to above in the section on the Presidency, is a device under which the federal government takes over the administration of a state, supplanting state authorities. The occasions for intervention provided in the constitutions are in reality interpreted broadly so as to cover any conceivable situation.

IV   *Policy*

A. THE MAKING OF POLICY

In CONSTITUTIONAL states functioning according to principles of the separation of powers, one might expect the flow of policy in the process of formation to move in a course suggested by the sequence of the topics dealt with to this point: groups-parties-legislature-executive-judiciary. In other words, policy could be expected to originate in the needs of specific population groups, arising against a background of a given political culture and state of public opinion; from this starting point should derive the programs, personnel, and policy orientations of the political parties, which, through the channels of legislative action, frame projects of law to answer those needs; the implementation of the laws approved by the legislature rests, in turn, with the executive authorities, limited, it may be, by judicial determinations.

The premise that has guided the relative emphasis placed on the different elements in the material this book covers has been based on a rather different conception of the process of policy-making. Policy, in this view, is set principally in the direct interaction of executive (that is, President) and groups; the other agencies that are formally involved in the process play a quite secondary and often negligible role. The pattern is of this nature: policy is set by the President on the basis of his conception of public needs and of personal ideals and goals of his own; it is retracted, modified, or extended on the basis of groups' reactions aimed directly at the President—in "behind the scenes" access to him personally, leading to efforts at persuasion, intimidation, or bribery; and in strikes, lockouts, demonstrations, riots, and threats of revolution and *coup d'état*. The role of legislature and judiciary is minimized, that of groups is augmented; while the parties serve principally to call the signals for group direct action.

Fidel Castro's "direct democracy," his enunciation of new policies in the course of an oration to a sympathetic crowd that shouts appropriate responses, is thus a kind of caricature of the processes by which policy is actually made in the countries of the area.

Let us now turn to examine some of the substantive problems of policy-making. Because of the evident limitations of space, the discussion below will be confined to the major policy issue in contemporary Latin America: policy for economic development. The concluding section will tie together some of the major themes developed in the book in a treatment of "policy for political development."

B. POLICY FOR ECONOMIC DEVELOPMENT

THE NATURE OF THE PROBLEM

Economic issues are always central to politics, to be sure, but in present-day Latin America economic problems have taken on an especial urgency. The rate of population growth has accelerated, due in large part to the decrease in the death rate consequent on the adoption of preventive public health techniques, without any compensating reduction in the birth rate. In other words, it is not enough today for national production to grow; if it does not grow faster than population, then despite increased production, per capita levels of consumption deteriorate. There are ever more mouths to feed, backs to clothe, heads to shelter.

Not only are the problems themselves more acute, but the consciousness of their existence as problems for which remedies exist has been heightened by developments in communications and travel that repeatedly bring the suffering into confrontation with the comfortable. At the same time the evolution of the Soviet Union to a position from which its missionary message of material betterment may be heard with both force and plausibility acts as a catalyst in inducing readiness to bring about change—to some extent for the forces within the Latin American countries seeking amelioration of conditions; more strongly for those in the United States and in the local upper classes fearful primarily of the extension of Soviet influence.

The conditions that lead to low levels of production and low standards of living in Latin America might be summarized briefly as follows, bearing in mind always that here we are generalizing and therefore necessarily over-simplifying. In the agricultural sector, especially in the growing of food crops for local consumption, modern technique is generally not followed, production is not rationally organized, and incentives are lacking. The crops concentrated on for export are however also those being increasingly produced, often at lower cost, by the countries of Africa and Asia; this means the steady long-term depression of prices. At the same time, given the fairly inelastic demand curves that exist for these products,[1] short-term fluctuations in supply result in drastic shifts in world market prices, with a resultant inability to budget income over a longer period that renders rational planning extremely difficult.

Government policy, for its part, often does little to help. Taxation is often counterproductive (in the form of export taxes, as in the case of Paraguay, for example, which may be easy to collect, and dependable as a source of revenue, but limit sales of the country's products by raising the prices at which they are sold abroad). Tax policy is rarely set with a view to mobilizing capital and directing it where it will most aid development.

THE IMPERATIVES OF ECONOMIC DEVELOPMENT POLICY

One of the striking features of the current phase of Latin American history is that in embarking on programs of economic develop-

[1] That is, demand does not change much in response to changes in price; the price of coffee has to drop a great deal before Brazil can sell additional amounts abroad. I have been prevailed on not to discuss possible remedial action through international agreement—commodity agreements, free trade areas, etc.—which would take the discussion too far afield.

ment, governments of all sorts find that, regardless of their ideological orientations and policy preferences, the requirements of development impose certain imperatives of their own on the direction of policy.

This dynamic of the situation has had curious and spectacular results. The same Arturo Frondizi who helped undermine Perón's position with a powerful radio speech against the dictator's change of policy toward permitting the exploitation of Argentine oil resources by foreign companies, for example, can find himself, four years later, as President, inviting foreign oil interests to Argentina under favorable terms. Two years after commencing his term of office by decreeing a 60 per cent general increase in wages, he can find himself using the army to break strikes called to back up union wage demands.

Similarly, Juan Lechín Oquendo, the secretary-general of the Bolivian mineworkers' union and the country's Vice-President, formerly a Trotskyite and an "anti-Yankee" economic nationalist, can find himself on a pilgrimage to Washington early in 1961 to try to arrange for North American investment in Bolivia's ailing tin-mining industry. Clearly, one cannot argue with economics; one can only obey—or rather, one can disobey only at the price of unpleasant consequences. What, then, are these powerful and paradox-inducing imperatives that are imposed by a policy of economic development?

The *sine qua non* of economic development is investment. Development means the expansion of per capita production, year after year; that is, a steady increase in productivity, the capacity to produce. This increase has come about, in the developed countries, primarily through the increased use of machinery and the improvement of technique. This in turn means that current resources must be devoted, as much as possible, not to consumption—the purchase or manufacture of goods for immediate use—but to producer's goods —tools, machinery, commercial buildings, transportation capacity— which serve to increase future production.

One can raise investment funds either at home or abroad. We turn first to the problems of attracting foreign investment.

Foreign Investment. A policy of attracting investment from abroad is faced with several political difficulties. In Latin America especially, there is an emotional resentment of foreign investment as such, partly for historical reasons, partly based on economic misunderstanding, and partly based on genuine current grievances.

There is, first of all, the allegation that foreign investors interfere in the politics of the host country. Warrant for this charge can certainly be found in the history of the foreign relations of the Latin American states. In the early years of the twentieth century, foreign holders of the bonds issued by the various governments of the area were uniformly successful in inducing their own governments to intervene on their behalf, by diplomatic representations and on occasion by military action, when payment obligations on the bonds were not met. The "Roosevelt Corollary" to the Monroe Doctrine was occasioned by U. S. acknowledgement of the justice of the claims of the foreign bondholders, on the one hand, together with reluctance to see European powers intervene in the Western Hemisphere, on the other. The administrations of Theodore Roosevelt and Taft themselves took action to safeguard bondholders' interests by seizing customs houses (customs duties being at the time the chief source of public revenue) in Haiti, the Dominican Republic, and Nicaragua; these customs receiverships developed into full-scale military occupations, the last of which was not finally liquidated until 1934.

Direct government action carried to the point of overt military intervention on behalf of investors in the economy of another state is today, clearly, a thing of the past. The fact that United States investors cannot count on automatic government intervention on their behalf was demonstrated by the Roosevelt administration's policy of restraint toward the Mexican expropriation of foreign oil interests in 1938. Nevertheless, the defense of investors' interests, along with the protection of its citizens in their other activities abroad, remains a routine concern of any foreign office; damage to those interests invariably occasions protest, and may result in a general deterioration of relations between the states concerned.

Of course, foreign companies have been known to interfere in local politics on their own without calling in the help of the home government. This type of practice occurred in most flagrant form during the early years of the present century, and the latter part of the nineteenth, perhaps with Samuel Zemurray (at the time, of Standard Fruit) the most notorious offender. Foreign companies no longer begin civil wars and equip one of the contending armies, as Zemurray is reputed to have done, but it would be unrealistic to suppose that they do not try to foster and protect their interests by political activities, just as domestic companies do.

One should not go to the other extreme, however, and think that foreign economic interests, today, "give orders" to local governments. Competent and responsible governments can dictate to foreign companies the terms on which they will operate locally, with the companies' only recourse to close down operations if the terms are too harsh; the government in power in 1958 in Venezuela revised in its own favor the arrangements under which foreign oil companies operated, for example, while Costa Rica, Panama, and Honduras have taken similar action with relation to the banana companies. A corrupt and irresponsible political leadership may still be bribed by a foreign operator to accept unfavorable terms; but surely in such a case the fault lies only partly with the company.

Even during the period when the ownership of government bonds of the Latin American states by individuals and financial institutions was a major category of foreign investment in the area, direct economic activity by foreign companies took place, principally in mining and the development of railroads. Direct investment today is concentrated in two types of activity: the development of primary production—of crops and minerals, that is—for the export market; and, more recently, in the manufacture of consumer goods and the provision of services for the local market. Each of these types of activities has generated its own characteristic set of resentments on the part of the Latin American populations.

In relation to the exploitation of mineral resources for export— oil, metals, nitrates—the rather curious idea has evolved, somewhat

similar to the attitude of a misguided wing of the North American
conservation movement, that the "taking out" of the country of its
natural resources for use elsewhere represents a kind of theft of the
national patrimony. This attitude can be encountered in Argentina
toward the foreign development of domestic oil deposits, for example, but it is general, at a popular level, throughout the area. In
economic terms this belief makes no sense, of course: a resource
lying untouched under the ground is without value—especially since
technological developments may in any case render its use obsolete
at some future date. The nation clearly benefits, in wages, tax
revenues, government participation in the enterprise's profits, and a
raising of the general level of economic activity, by the exploitation
of the resource.

A further component of the generally unfavorable attitude to
foreign investment common in the area is the feeling, comparable
to one of the premises of Marxist economics, that any return on
capital represents unjust exploitation; that only labor creates value
and therefore the interest and profits accruing to the provider of
capital represents an unearned charge on the economy. From the
viewpoint of capitalist economics, of course, this attitude misses the
point: capital is a scarce resource and so must be attracted by a rate
of compensation adequate to meet those offered by the competing
demands for capital.

In addition, there are frequently present various specific grievances
against individual foreign companies. One, the factual basis for
which is disappearing among the more enlightened foreign companies, lies in the differential treatment of local and foreign employees in salaries, fringe benefits, and advancement to responsible
positions. Another, applying specifically to utilities companies, is
directed against the rates charged, rate increases being clearly visible
and of widespread impact, and also against the quality of the service
provided; complaints on the latter score are quite likely to be well-
founded, by the way.

One charge sometimes made against a foreign company engaged
in the production of the single crop on the export of which the

country's economy largely depends is that its activities maintain the monocultural system with all the evils that attend it. It is difficult to see any justice in this charge, however, which amounts in effect to blaming the company for what other companies and individuals are *not* doing; except in the case that its activities actually prevent the economy from diversifying—if, for example, it monopolizes the country's land or other strategic resources. In such a case—as in others where a foreign company may justifiably bear blame—the local government is usually equally at fault for allowing a disadvantageous system to continue. Where competent, honest, and responsible governments exist, abuses of their position by foreign companies disappear quickly.

Such governments are unfortunately not the rule in Latin America as yet, and the suspicion of venal practice automatically attaches to government leaders whose relations with foreign business interests are close. Where a government tries to attract foreign investment by means of tax or other concessions, for example, a substantial segment of the population is ready to assume immediately that politicians have been bribed by foreign interests to make the concession in question.

Given the set of popular attitudes described, it is clear that substantial political pitfalls await governments that encourage foreign investment. The unpopularity of Perón's decision—after the deleterious effects of his economic policies had begun to make themselves felt—to invite North American companies to exploit Argentine oil deposits helped create the climate of opinion that contributed to his downfall. In this respect, as in others, Mexico's leadership has shown itself skilled and resourceful in developing a rational alternative to such self-defeating but popular gestures of economic nationalism, in the form of "Mexicanization." "Mexicanization"[2] means that no economic enterprise operating in Mexico may be controlled by foreigners; in other words, that decisions affecting the Mexican economy must be made only by Mexicans. This formulation clearly appeals to economic nationalism; but what the policy means in

[2] Not to be confused with nationalization.

practice is that at least 51 per cent of the stock of an enterprise must be owned by Mexicans. The only damage to the Mexican economy that might arise under this formula is that investments advantageous to the economy for which foreign capital was available might not be made because of a shortage of matching Mexican capital. In practice, this does not occur. The effect instead has been to channel Mexican capital into productive enterprise rather than non-productive by providing attractive investment opportunities in enterprises organized by reputable foreign firms manufacturing or marketing established products. It may also have been the case that the foreign capital available for investment in Mexico went twice as far as it would otherwise have done, whereas at the same time the sting was taken out of the irrational appeals of economic nationalism. Mexico's example is likely to be followed elsewhere. Tunisia has already adopted a similar law, and one is under discussion in Brazil.

It remains true, nevertheless, that the encouragement of foreign investment—chiefly, of course, North American—is a suspect or unpopular policy in Latin America.

Promoting Domestic Investment. One raises funds at home by forcing the reduction or postponement of consumption—this is the net effect of a government policy aimed at amassing capital for investment, regardless of the specific technique chosen. One can hold down wages, thus making funds available for business to invest itself; one can raise taxes, thus giving government an investable "surplus"; or one can create new currency by inflationary techniques (for example, printing new bills), which is similar in effect to a highly arbitrary tax—it makes money available to government by taking purchasing power from those groups and individuals that are least able to protect themselves against inflation.

The inflationary road represents the path of least resistance for governments desiring to raise funds. Its effects are not so immediately felt, and thus opposition not so easily aroused as by a wage freeze or a tax rise. As we shall see below, inflation has side effects that damage the prospects for development. Nevertheless, a certain amount of inflation is probably unavoidable in a developing economy. The problem is to try to hold it to a minimum.

Given the sheer magnitude of the task of developing the economies of Latin America, especially in view of the pressures of population rise, all potential sources of investment funds must be mobilized. Although this fact appears clear enough to an outsider, too many Latin Americans fall into the painless fallacy of assuming that the United States can inject enough dollars to do the job by itself. The Alliance for Progress program is clear on this point: the Latin American states cannot expect the United States to supply investment funds so long as domestic sources of genuinely surplus funds remain untapped.

It is not to be denied that there are indeed local funds in the countries of the area that are not being used to further development, even though they could be diverted to this use without causing any hardship whatsoever. The legendary anonymous Swiss bank accounts still play their part in absorbing the funds misappropriated by the betrayers of the public trust who are found all too frequently in the Latin American republics. Many Latin American investors put their money into securities of United States firms, presumably for safety's sake. Moreover, where those able to do so do invest in their own country's economy, the fields chosen are rarely the productive ones. For example, a typical contemporary use of investment funds is in the construction of luxury apartment buildings and hotels.

At the same time, some of the funds that might otherwise be used for investment are not invested at all but instead are expended on luxury items imported from abroad. This phenomenon constitutes not only a diminution of potential investment, but also a burden on the country's limited supply of foreign currencies, which would better be devoted to the import of goods that can aid the process of development.

Here clearly the nation will benefit from policies which seek to channel funds of this type into investment rather than consumption, and which conserve foreign exchange for the import of machinery and other items of strategic value for a development program. Tax and exchange control policies are appropriate tools for these purposes.

Monetary Stabilization. As was noted above, the danger of inflation is very great during the initial stages of a development program. Money is being spent on capital projects; that is, workers are receiving wages for constructing roads, buildings, and dams, none of which they can buy. The money they receive goes to buy the limited amount of consumers' goods available, and prices rise; an inflationary spiral begins. Accordingly, an anti-inflationary program, designed to maintain a stable value for the currency, is a necessary part of a policy for economic development. Without such a program, costs rise, and the development plan must be curtailed.

Furthermore, such investment as does take place during a period of continuing inflation will be misplaced, from the point of view of economic development, since it will be designed to be proof against future price rises. Here the luxury-apartment-house problem enters. If one invests in a factory, say, one can raise prices as inflation proceeds; but costs of labor and raw materials can be expected to rise, and minimize or wipe out profits. An apartment house, on the other hand, needs very little continuing expenditure —its chief cost is in the original construction. Thus the problem of rising costs is minimized, whereas rents can be steadily raised as inflation proceeds. An inflationary situation thus tends to channel investment, where that takes place, into non-productive uses.

A monetary stabilization program of this type needs to be introduced at other times too, of course, not only in conjunction with a development policy; during the last decade perhaps half of the Latin American countries have had to undertake rigorous stabilization programs, usually in cooperation with the International Monetary Fund, whose purpose it is to promote the continuing free convertibility of currencies.

What governmental actions are called for by the inauguration of a policy for monetary stabilization? Essentially, one must prevent rises in wages and prices, and reduce government expenditures to the level of income or below—that is, one must balance the budget. Although the elimination of inflation will lead to general benefits in the long run, a stabilization program indisputably imposes hardships and even suffering while it is first taking effect. Inflation is like a toothache, which hurts steadily, and is at the same time the symptom of an unhealthy condition which, if unattended, will lead to further physical deterioration. A stabilization program is like the extraction of an aching tooth, which may hurt excruciatingly while it is in progress, will require subsequent readjustment, but in the long run —if it is successful, and it may not be—is better both for health and for comfort.

Some typical features of recent stabilization programs in Latin America, which illustrate their unpopularity and thus the political dangers which they occasion, have been the following. A leading feature of the program embarked on by President Frondizi of Argentina was a freeze on wages, and he carried this to the point of calling out troops to break up violent demonstrations arising out of strikes staged in support of wage demands. The consequent difficulties he found in attempting a rapprochement with organized labor, and the support union members continued to vouchsafe to the neo-Peronists, were at the root of the action of the military in removing him from office in April of 1962.

The government of Jânio Quadros in Brazil attempted to pursue a policy of monetary stabilization that would repair the damage caused by the acute inflation that took place during the term of his predecessor, Juscelino Kubitschek. Among other features, the program involved the discharge of many government employees, and reductions in the pay of others, in the attempt to halt the printing of new currency that was the easy way out of its problems favored by the previous administration. President Quadros resigned his post, apparently in the unsuccessful attempt to get the Congress to vote him full legislative powers with which to implement his economic policies.

In Bolivia, the administration of President Siles Zuazo (1956-60) found itself under continual popular siege, as it were, in response to the President's attempt to halt the inflation that had sent the value of the boliviano from 1.5 to the dollar to 12,000 to the dollar in 20 years, and which had reached a runaway pace during the term of his predecessor. The Siles administration, in cooperation with the International Monetary Fund, not only tried to hold the line on wage increases for workers, including those in the government-owned tin mines, which clearly meant hardship for them and their families, but also removed most of the subsidies it had been making to hold down the prices of items for sale in the miners' commissaries. President Siles even resorted on two occasions to hunger strikes, in the courageous, and eventually successful, attempt to shame workers into giving up their wage demands, while demonstrating to the IMF the sincerity of his attempt to bring about monetary stabilization. This was a tragic situation for all concerned. There can be little doubt of the abject conditions of life of the miners, as indeed of most of the rest of the population of that unhappy country. From this point of view, their claims were certainly justified. Yet the state of the economy, and especially of the tin mines themselves, was such that it could not support any improvement in those conditions. If the stabilization program were successful, foreign financing could be obtained and used to advantage, it was hoped, in an attempt to rehabilitate the mines and begin the long climb to decent standards of life for the Bolivian people. This was a case of a very painful toothache, but also of an extremely painful extraction, with the prospect of a lengthy and problematical recovery.

POLITICAL PROBLEMS OF POLICY FOR ECONOMIC DEVELOPMENT

At the turn of the century a President named Porfirio Díaz was in office in Mexico, together with a group of technical aides who have gone down in history as the *científicos*. They earned the name by having as their intention to govern Mexico scientifically, that is, to allow their policies to be guided by the technical requirements of political and fiscal statecraft. The *científicos* were concerned that

Mexico's economy develop, and they embarked on programs adapted to this end, given what they believed to be the scientific knowledge of the time. Foreign investment was, of course, necessary, and was heavily favored by the laws. Drawing on the contemporary dogmas of what they took to be the scientific study of society, the government determined to enter upon no programs of social amelioration, which would destroy the autonomy of the marketplace (economics) and encourage idleness and immorality (sociology); although in any case no improvement could be wrought in the Indian, who was biologically inferior material (anthropology). Thus, the regime followed an authoritarian policy of repressing discontent while allowing very liberal concessions to foreign business interests—Mexico became "the mother of foreigners, the stepmother of Mexicans."

The danger of a new Porfirianism lurks in contemporary economic development policies, too. It is easy to interpret the technical requirements of a development program that includes monetary stabilization features as a purely "Right-wing" program designed in the class interest of the rich—easy, that is, for rich and poor alike. As was previously stated, such a program can be expected to entail such measures as a freeze on wages, a decrease in government spending on welfare programs, the reduction of the number of government employees and a lowering of the pay of the remainder, the maintenance or even imposition of taxes on the poor, together with the adoption of policies favorable to foreign and domestic investors. It is only natural that the well-to-do will embrace the program, protesting that they regret the necessity of receiving benefits for themselves while hardships are imposed on the poor, but that they make the sacrifice in the interest of developing the country; whereas the poor immediately see that what must have happened is that the government leaders have sold out to the bankers of Wall Street.

A development program in a free economy readily takes on a character of this kind; and not only in a free economy: the economic development of the Soviet Union, which proceeded almost entirely without foreign assistance, entailed greater sacrifices from the poor, especially from the peasants, than could have been imposed by a democratic government.

Two lines of policy are open to responsible democratic governments to soften these "Right-wing" effects of the development program. One is to lay stress on the "Left" measures that assist development; these exist, although to a lesser extent than those of Rightist implications. A measure of this kind already referred to is to limit the importation of luxury consumer's goods. Another is the expansion of educational facilities and programs, which can be regarded as a high-return investment in human beings. Another is land reform, which is taken up at greater length later.

The other line of policy is simply to conduct a program of social amelioration which does not in itself conduce to economic development—which will in fact, taken by itself, damage the development program, because it diverts resources that could otherwise have been used in investment. To embark on a social welfare program, in this context, means to slow development, other things being equal. Several observations need to be made on this point, however. One is that the purpose of the whole economic development policy is to raise standards for future generations; to adopt social welfare measures today slows the rate of progress but seems eminently just in that it ensures that the present generation will derive benefits from the process also. Clearly, one must not overdo expenditures on current programs, however, since it is possible to slow the rate of development to zero or to a negative figure, as was the case during the administration of Juan Perón.

Another argument may carry more force in this connection, however. Given the fact of political instability, it is quite feasible that the political disorder following on the consistent implementation of a purely "Rightist" development policy may cause the failure of the whole program—either by forcing a change of government or simply by itself consuming resources. For example: the government of Cheddi Jagan in British Guiana embarked on a development program at a maximum rate of speed, which called for sacrifices so unpopular that the costs of the destruction caused by the ensuing riots will set back the development program by two or three years. One is reminded of the man who proposed to save money by feeding his horse less; he saved a lot of money, but the horse died. One can develop an economy mightily only to have it collapse for "extraneous," but avoidable, reasons.

Taking this into consideration, it becomes clear that spending on housing, social services, etc., may actually be a rational charge on the economic development program, even in an accounting sense, if without it political disturbance would make the economic effort impossible or impose additional internal policing costs on the government.

LAND REFORM

Under the circumstances of land tenure most general in Latin America, a policy of land reform can provide the attractive prospect of at the same time promoting economic development, bringing about an immediate rise in living standards, fostering national integration, augmenting the government's popularity, reducing political violence, and contributing to human dignity. Whether these possibilities will all become actual depends, however, on the successful surmounting of a variety of obstacles.

Land reform means the transfer of the ownership of land to those who work it. Given the mode in which the overwhelming majority of the large estates of the southern part of the hemisphere are farmed, this can be expected to result in an increase of production; people work better when they are working for themselves, and not for others. If this occurs, production goes up, and the peasant eats better; he may have a surplus for sale, which goes to the city to feed workers in a new industry, perhaps; and so on. Now, several limitations of land reform need to be noted right away. One is that some crops, as we have seen, are rationally farmed on a large-scale basis; production drops if land in these crops is broken up into small parcels. Because of this, the Mexican land reform has retained intact some extremely large production units planted in cotton and hemp. The same comment applies to estates that are being rationally farmed with the aid of mechanized equipment. The latter constitute, however, a very small proportion of Latin American agricultural units.

For many reasons, it is easy for a land reform to fail completely. For example: the peasant needs to buy tools, seed, and fertilizer; he needs to feed his family; but he gets no income from his plot until the harvest. If the government does not provide credit at the same time as it distributes land, then the new landowner has to go into debt to the local moneylender, mortgaging his farm, say, until the harvest. Local rates of interest are exorbitant, becoming astronomical in some areas. If there is a crop failure, the peasant loses his land to the holder of the mortgage—and in the course of one or two generations the land becomes again concentrated in a few hands.

So provision must be made for credit facilities at the time of the land distribution. Agricultural extension services need to be provided, too, to acquaint the new smallholder with modern farm technique, if the government expects maximum agricultural production as an aid in the country's development program.

The Mexican, and now the Cuban, land reforms have partly eliminated the problem of reconcentration by limiting the scope of ownership of the distributed lands. In Mexico, the reform has (with ups and downs over the years) stressed the *ejido,* the system of village landholding in common. Under this system the land belongs to the village as a whole; the individual has a limited title to his plot, farming it and owning its produce but forbidden to dispose of the land. In Cuba the regime has begun establishing state farms alongside the individual and collective-holdings systems; in them the peasant is a worker employed by the state, and an owner only in the nominal sense that all citizens are owners of public concerns.

Problems also exist in connection with the compensation given to owners of the land. The Indian peasants who seize lands belonging to absentee landowners in the highlands of Peru don't perceive the existence of a problem here: the land has always been theirs but was simply taken from them by force at the time of the Conquest. This argument carries a certain amount of conviction. Nevertheless, the present owners do have a legal right to the land, which entitles them to compensation if the land is taken from them. Clearly, the government cannot pay cash on the land it expropriates; this would introduce a great deal of currency into the economy without a compensating increase in production, which means inflation. One can pay in bonds, instead of in cash—but if the bond does not mature for a long time (40 years, say), and meanwhile pays only 2 per cent interest, the landowner is getting very little indeed for his property. The issue of compensation thus becomes one of degree: how much should be paid, over what time span, and in what proportion payments should be made in cash. An arrangement very fair to the landowners—perhaps too fair, since it puts a strain on the national treasury—is that adopted in the Venezuelan land reform law of 1960, which in most cases provides for compensation one-third in cash, and two-thirds in long-term bonds.

The problem of fixing a price on the land to be expropriated can also create difficulties. The Guatemalan land reform of 1952, for example, took as its basis the assessed value of the holdings, which represented only a fraction of their market value.

Now that the Alliance for Progress program is in existence, and stipulates agrarian reform as one of the requirements a country must satisfy in order to receive U. S. aid, one has to beware of nominal agrarian reforms that on detailed inspection turn out to be no more than old-fashioned "boondoggles." Such a pseudo-reform might involve, say, the landowner's disposing of the barren sections of his property to the government (represented by his cousin, an official in the land reform agency) at an inflated price. In view of the fate of other well-conceived programs in Latin America, this kind of thing is far from being out of the question.

It is possible, nevertheless, for a responsible government to put through a land reform program that works, although the difficulties are substantial. If such a program is successful, it can not only raise the living standards of those directly involved, but also contribute to the economic growth of the country as a whole; it can give the peasants a new dignity and pride in themselves, while at the same time integrating their activities into the national economy and national life.

Whether a land reform program is feasible depends in part on the availability of arable land. Many of the countries of Latin America have unused land, at present inaccessible but usable if access roads are constructed. This is not the case in all of the republics, however. In Haiti, for example, where land ownership is already widely distributed, the problem is simply one of population density. There are just too many people for the available land, and as a result individual holdings are very small indeed.

The institution of the Alliance for Progress program, with its clearly announced intention of putting "strings" in the form of requirements for tax, land, and administrative reform, on United States aid to her southern neighbors, has placed new emphasis on one aspect of the policy-making process in the typical Latin American state. This is its responsiveness to foreign, as well as to domestic, constituencies. To be sure, it is true today that every small state —and every large one too, for that matter—must take into account the probable reactions from other countries to measures it contemplates taking. But the Latin American states, dependent as most of them are on the world market for their products and on the need for foreign investment, are under special constraints on this score. One hopes that the resentment that the need to consider foreign views may engender will be mollified if the fulfillment of prior conditions for Alliance for Progress aid is monitored by an inter-American agency like the Economic and Social Committee of the Organization of American States, as the Charter of Punta del Este provides, rather than by the United States directly. The necessity for some monitoring of performance remains, however.

C. IN CONCLUSION: POLICY FOR POLITICAL DEVELOPMENT

THE PROBLEM IN PERSPECTIVE

Earlier in the book the concept of "political development" was introduced, to mean the evolution of social and political practice through stages correlating increasingly with both democracy and stability. Such evolution can come about through the emergence of secular economic and demographic trends; unbidden, increments in political development may arrive on the crests of waves of immigration, or be found on the peaks of economic booms. At the same time, it should be possible for political leaders to pursue policies deliberately designed to promote political development, just as today they feel they must adopt programs that will encourage economic development.

This has in fact occurred. As one looks at the countries that stand toward the "more advanced" end of the spectrum of political development in this light, it becomes clear that in several cases their favorable situation is due not only to advantageous economic and demographic factors, although these exist, but often to the deliberate action of some creative statesman who diagnosed his country's ills and brought about structural changes designed to remedy them. In Mexico, for example, Plutarco Elías Calles knew perfectly well what he was doing when he created the National Revolutionary Party in the wake of Obregón's assassination. In the radio speech Calles made explaining his move, he made clear that the formation of the party was an attempt to assure the peaceful succession to power while at the same time maintaining the social and economic goals of the Revolution, by making the transition from the era of personalism to the era of institutionalism.[3]

José Batlle y Ordóñez played a similar role in the history of Uruguay, although the manner of his approach was quite different. Batlle's place in Uruguayan history is due to his three great achievements: he ended the civil warfare between Colorados and Blancos that had been endemic until his Presidency; he was the architect of Uruguayan democratic socialism and the welfare state; and he introduced the idea of the collegial executive as a device to avoid the danger of dictatorship inherent in the institution of the strong Presi-

[3] Most observers have been rather skeptical of Calles' motivation here, interpreting his action in the light of his later behavior as "strong man." For reasons too complex to go into here, I am inclined to accept Calles' stated motives at face value.

dency. Under Batlle's guidance, Uruguay, too, took a giant step along the road to the goal of a stability that was combined with democracy and at the same time with social reform.

Alberto Lleras Camargo has attempted the same feat in Colombia, using still other methods. Hoping to put an end to party warfare and stabilize the succession to power by the National Front agreement, which provides for parity of the Conservatives and Liberals on all political bodies and the alternation of the Presidency between the parties, Lleras's success in the long run will depend on how well the National Front can satisfy popular demands for social and economic amelioration.

Judging by the features common to the examples given above, one could say that successful policies for political development of the past have (1) reduced the scope and intensity of conflict among parties and organized groups; (2) stabilized the succession to high office, while limiting the possibilities of the abuse of powers; and (3) promoted programs of social and economic welfare.

COMPLEMENTARY PERSPECTIVES ON THE PROBLEM

Subsidiary conclusions arrived at in other sections of the book converge on this definition of the basic problem of promoting political development as involving the attainment of an inter-group *modus vivendi,* the stabilization of democratic political institutions, and the adoption of a liberal social and economic policy as a permanent national goal; these are the three dimensions in which a high level of political development is attained. These three aspects are not separable from each other, but act in mutual support and reinforcement.

A thesis of this kind was implicit in the discussion of techniques for curbing the military influence in politics. It was remarked then that the best defense against the military ultimatum was in the last analysis popular support in the sense of willingness on the part of the general public to fight on behalf of the regime, whether or not actual fighting proved to be necessary. But the availability of such popular support depends after all on the government's pursuance

of a generally accepted social policy that acknowledges the legitimate claims on government of the major population sectors, and
especially—as we noted in the case of Mexico—of those able to use
violence effectively. From the point of view of the groups to which
the weapon of violence is available, they can forgo its use only on
the assurance of a continuing respected voice in the processes of
decision-making, an institutionalized place in an authentically constitutional state. The preservation of civilian supremacy, then, rests
in a general sense on the regime's social policy, and on its representative character.

Similarly, from the individual's point of view, it is clear that loyalty to a system of government depends on the ability of that system
to satisfy needs felt to be legitimate. Loyalty to constitutional forms
in themselves certainly exists, but with the marked tendency of being
considered secondary to the protection of one's concrete interests.[4]
Put briefly: one defends an order of things in which one has a stake.
Herein lies the connection between political stability and social
reform, which becomes clearer if one considers the political effects
of land reform. Farmers, as experience everywhere shows, can be
either very radical or very conservative. One way to shift peasants
from one end of the political spectrum to another, to make conservatives out of revolutionaries, is by giving them the land they work,
converting proletarians into propertyholders.[5]

From yet another perspective: that general acknowledgement of
the legitimacy of a regime that is the best long-run assurance of
stability can come today, given present-day attitudes, only when
institutions are founded on principles of democracy and social welfare; in other words, where all population elements have a voice in
policy, and government fosters the well-being of all.

A policy for political development, to summarize, involves the
pacification of the major population groups by conferring on each

[4] This is clearly visible in the United States in attitudes toward the Supreme
Court. The conservative who defended the Court's constitutional role when
it was nullifying New Deal legislation attacks it when it outlaws segregation.

[5] A good illustration of this is the change in the political attitudes of the
peasantry during the French Revolution.

of them a role in the institutionalized processes of decision-making and a stake in a socioeconomic order constructed along equitable lines. There is no incompatibility, at this level, between the goals of democracy, stability, and welfare; to the statesman's eye they blend into a single historic aim.

It is possible to meet these historic needs spuriously, to make a show of their attainment that is really a false one, capable, in the long run, only of retarding genuine political evolution. This possibility, in our time, has been raised by the Peronistas on the Right and the Fidelistas on the Left. But their claims to satisfy the needs of the time are based on force and fraud. The regime of each purchases what stability it has only with the use of force, however discriminatingly or intermittently it is used; the claim of each to be "truly" democratic, without fair elections and civil liberties, clearly rests on fraud—on misrepresentation and double-talk; their ability to satisfy the people's economic requirements rests on fraud in the one case and force in the other—Perón created a transient lower-class prosperity that was based on consuming capital and thus could not last; Fidel Castro will probably succeed, if he remains in power, in raising the living standards of the Cuban peasants, but he will be able to maintain himself through the interim period of dislocation attendant on the conversion to an operating socialist economy only through the extensive use of coercion, which will become a need that feeds on itself.

The existence of the spurious and the genuine answers to the needs of the historic moment provides at the same time the danger and the hope—taken together, the challenge—of Latin American politics in our time.

Suggested for Further Reading

Bemis, Samuel Flagg, *The Latin American Policy of the United States,* Harcourt Brace, New York, 1943. Detailed history, favorable to the United States.

Christensen, Asher N., ed., *The Evolution of Latin American Government,* Holt, New York, 1951. Readings from leading scholars.

Crawford, William Rex, *A Century of Latin American Thought,* Harvard, Cambridge, 1944. First-rate intellectual history.

Davis, Harold E., ed., *Government and Politics in Latin America,* Ronald, New York, 1958. Treatment by topics.

Ferguson, J. Halcro, *Latin America: The Balance of Race Redressed,* Oxford, London, 1961. Brief survey of race relations.

Gomez, Rosendo A., *Latin American Government and Politics,* Random House, New York, 1960. Capsule treatment, with stress on the colonial background and the Presidency.

Hanke, Lewis, *Latin America: Continent in Ferment,* 2 vols., Van Nostrand, Princeton, 1960. Succinct surveys by country.

Hanson, Simon G., *Economic Development in Latin America,* Inter-American Affairs Press, Washington, 1951.

Johnson, John J., *Political Change in Latin America,* Stanford, 1958. An interesting interpretation of developments since 1900 in several key countries.

Lieuwen, Edwin, *Arms and Politics in Latin America,* rev. ed., Praeger, New York, 1961.

Mecham, J. Lloyd, *Church and State in Latin America,* University of North Carolina Press, Chapel Hill, 1934.

Pierson, William W., and Gil, Federico G., *Governments of Latin America,* McGraw-Hill, New York, 1957. Solid treatment by topics.

Porter, Charles O., and Alexander, Robert J., *The Struggle for Democracy in Latin America,* Macmillan, New York, 1961. Interpretive contemporary history.

Schurz, William Lytle, *Latin America: A Descriptive Survey,* Dutton, New York, 1949.

Index

NOTE:

Hispanic surnames are sometimes "composite," that is, both father's and mother's family names are used. Thus the family name of Adolfo López Michelsen is *López;* his father's name was Alfonso López Pumarejo. Accordingly, both would be found listed under *L.* In addition, some family names are themselves "composite," and a double surname is handed down through the male line, for example, Miró Quesada, a famous family name in Peru. The situation is further complicated because many political figures do not normally use the mother's name; others use more than one *Christian* name; still others, especially in Brazil but also elsewhere, are known commonly by their Christian names only. The hapless speaker of English just has to get used to this as best he can. The author's favorite example of the diversity with which one can be confronted is a poster he saw in Lima urging the voters to support the APRA ticket in the 1962 elections. The names of the party's candidates for President and First and Second Vice-Presidents were listed thus:

VICTOR RAUL

MANUEL SEOANE

ARCA PARRO

The top line gives the Christian names of the party's Presidential candidate, Haya de la Torre; the middle line gives the Christian name and the family name of the candidate for First Vice-President; the bottom line gives the composite surname of the third man on the party ticket.

186
Index